Reclaiming Ourselves

BOOKS BY SUSAN SHAPIRO BARASH

A PASSION FOR MORE: WIVES REVEAL THE AFFAIRS
   THAT MAKE OR BREAK THEIR MARRIAGES

SISTERS: DEVOTED OR DIVIDED

THE MEN OUT THERE: A WOMAN'S LITTLE BLACK
   BOOK

SECOND WIVES: THE PITFALLS AND REWARDS OF
   MARRYING WIDOWERS AND DIVORCED MEN

INVENTING SAVANNAH (fiction)

MOTHERS-IN-LAW AND DAUGHTERS-IN-LAW:
   LOVE, HATE, RIVALRY, AND RECONCILIATION

Reclaiming Ourselves

how women dispel
a legacy of bad choices

❧

Susan Shapiro Barash

❧

Berkeley Hills Books
Berkeley California

BERKELEY HILLS BOOKS, PUBLISHERS
PO Box 9877, Berkeley CA 94709
www.berkeleyhills.com

Printed by Data Reproductions, Auburn Hills MI

Distributed to the trade by Publishers Group West

Cover design by Hicks Studio, Berkeley CA

Photo © Alonzo Boldin

Library of Congress Cataloging-in-Publication Data

Barash, Susan Shapiro, 1954-
  Reclaiming ourselves : how women dispel a legacy of bad
choices /
Susan Shapiro Barash.
      p. cm.
  ISBN 1-893163-29-6 (perm. paper)
  1. Women--Psychology. 2. Passivity (Psychology) I. Title.
  HQ1206 .B22 2001
  305.4--dc21

                                    2001004449

for Gary

Acknowledgements

As always, I am very grateful to my three children, Jennie, Michael, and Elizabeth Ripps for their love and understanding. I thank my parents, Selma and Herbert L. Shapiro, as well as family members and friends. My father deserves special mention for his outstanding research skills.

I thank my editor, Rob Dobbin, at Berkeley Hills Books, for his trust in this project. In the world of publishing, I thank Richard Grossinger, Lori Ames, Cynthia Vartan, Debra Sloan, and Sarah Gallick. I thank Robert Marcus, my attorney, for his wise counsel and endless energy. At Marymount Manhattan College I thank Suzanne M. Murphy, Lewis Burke Frumkes, Scott Rubin, Joe Pospisil, Brendan Murphy, Carol Camper, Richard Hutzer, and the staff in the Development Office. My student assistants, Emilie Domer and Ryan Lonergan, did a terrific job. And thanks to Karen Wilder for her computer expertise.

The professionals who contributed to this book are impressive: Brondi Borer, a New York City divorce attorney; Dr. Ronnie Burak, a clinical psychologist with a practice in Jacksonville, Florida; Dr. Michaele Goodman, a clinical psychologist with a practice in New York City and Westchester; Dr. Michele Kasson, a psychologist who practices in New York City and Long Island and staff member of the Lifeline Center for Child Development; Anne Marie Keyes, Chair of the Philosophy Department at Marymount Manhattan College; Alice Michaeli, a sociologist whose specialty is marriage and the family and who teaches at SUNY; Antoinette Michaels, ACSW, the founder and director of the Hope Counseling Center in Sayville, New York; interfaith minister Katherine Rabinowitz, a nationally certified psychotherapist with a private practice in New York City; Amy Reisen, a matrimonial lawyer who practices in Milburn, New Jersey; and Brenda Szulman, CSW, who is certified in marital therapy and specializes in Anxiety and Depressive Orders.

I am extremely grateful to those women who have expressed their deepest feelings and personal evolution. They cannot be thanked by name because all identifying characteristics have been changed to insure confidentiality, and some characters are composites.

Finally, I thank my husband, Gary A. Barash, who understands why I write.

"…I was much too far out all my life
And not waving but drowning."

−Stevie Smith, "Not Waving but Drowning"

"Is a dream a lie if it don't come true
Or is it something worse?"

−Bruce Springsteen, "The River"

CONTENTS

Preface by Antoinette Michaels, ACSW *xiii*

Introduction 1

One The Princess Falls Asleep 11

Two Early Myths and How We Lose Our Way 29

Three The Lull of Love and a Material World 49

Four In the Driver's Seat: The Affair 83

Five Uncharted Waters: Divorce and Singlehood 113

Six Reinvention / Remarriage 139

Seven Mothering: Choices In and Out of Reality 165

Eight Missing Links / Friends and Family 195

Nine Confusion in our Careers / Financial Sleep 227

Ten Inheritance: Ourselves 255

References 263

Preface
by Antoinette Michaels, ACSW

It is time for many women to awaken from their slumber. Some-where between childhood and adulthood, many become lost to their own dreams and desires. It is as if they have forgotten who they really are. To wake up is to see past the conditioning of our society and our families. To wake up is to reclaim our true selves.

Being a psychotherapist and hypnotherapist for nearly twenty years, I have noticed a phenomenon among many of my women clients. My observation is that these women suffer from faulty perception and a denial of self. There is an inabil-ity to see things clearly, including themselves and those closest to them.

When a person is in a trance, there is a narrowing of their focus and a selective taking in of the environment around them. Many of these women appear to be sleepwalking through their own lives. My clients were especially preoccupied with find-ing love and keeping it. They were preoccupied with looking good and people-pleasing. What seemed odd at times to me was that even people whom they admittedly didn't like, respect, or value, they attempted to please. For many of these women, in spite of their desire for love, peace, happiness, and success, their choices made it difficult for them to obtain and reach their desired goals. In essence, this "other-oriented" way of living diverted them from their aspirations and their true being.

When these women begin to wake up, usually after some crisis or "life quake," they may begin to sweep up the debris of their lives. This group of women is stunned to learn that this life that they have been living has not been their own.

The disconnection from one spirit is a subtle process which begins as little girls and follows women into adulthood. People-pleasing, not making waves, denying one's needs, and self-sacrificing—all are encouraged and promoted in our society. What I would term "divine discontent" has sent many women in midlife seeking help to try and make sense of the pain and emptiness of their everyday existence. Some therapists have named this stage of development "mid-life crisis." I see it as a "mid-life awakening" and the reclaiming of oneself.

We become blinded to the obstructions in our lives, to what holds us back. For example, a woman could be dating an alcoholic. Or she could be dating a misogynist. Instead of recognizing these men for who they really are, the woman becomes focused on the initial seduction and the good parts or "honeymoon" phase of the relationship. If this man is an abuser, the syndrome becomes one of a period of abuse, followed by the kiss-and-make-up stage. There is amnesia or denial of how abusive the relationship really is in order for this woman to get through. She does not acknowledge that three hours of peace followed by ten hours of abuse is not acceptable. Her rationalization is that she will hang in for the good part. She erases the bad from her mind and is not aware of how the abuse is affecting both her and her partner. The real danger is that a woman such as this is not living up to her full potential and has no order or serenity.

Ironically, when we ask women what they want in their lives, they will say, Peace and happiness. Yet the choices women make do not reflect this conscious decision, but in fact the opposite. If we want to be happy, we do not remain in an environment where there is negativity. Women hold onto jobs for a false sense of security, which translates into money. But when they swap creativity and peace of mind for financial security, and live in fear of leaving one job for a lesser one, it becomes a problem. This is when women become or remain unconscious of how their choice is affecting their life. They operate mechanically, out of habit, often in familiar but destructive habits, and work against their chance of personal growth and well-being.

I believe that many people do not achieve their full potential and might never enjoy life as productively as they can. Regardless of a woman's circumstances, if she is mature, she can transcend a problem, and maintain inner strength. There are plenty of positive moments in life, there is plenty of joy to experience. Instead, so many women say to themselves, Why me?

There are women that go to the grave, unfortunately, without waking up. For other women, their awakening occurs when the pain is too great and is no longer bearable. Certain situations trigger the awakening, such as when a husband or significant other leaves or dies and her life is altered. Sometimes a woman is unable to leave and her husband will take the initiative. The ending feels abrupt to her because she has slept through the failing relationship. Now she wakes up to the reality of being alone and becomes responsible for her actions. At this point, she may rediscover herself.

An all-too-common reason for women waking up is when the abuse in their lives is so intensified–financially, emotionally, or physically–that they can no longer hide from themselves or from others. The situation has escalated to such a destructive level that it becomes visible to family members and friends. In these situations, those who are close to the victim may help her to wake up and take stock of her life. If these close friends and family members are so valued and respected by her, they might be able to break through the barrier of denial. A part of the waking-up process is seeking help and finding some type of self-help group. There are many choices, such as group therapy or individual therapy, that can be a catalyst to waking up: CoDA (Co-Dependents Anonymous), Twelve Steps, organized religion, meditation, and prayer. Any or all of these sources of support help women greatly in their quest to change themselves and to become strong enough to change. The future choices are ours if only we are responsible to ourselves. Instead of allowing things to happen to us by being passive, we now become participants in our own lives.

I see this syndrome of "waking up" most often among women who are between the ages of forty and mid-fifty. Younger women seem to conduct their relationships with more self-awareness and, hopefully, more equality. With women in their late twenties to late thirties there are other issues, mostly because these women are so influenced by a material world. Material goods, prestige, and power take precedence in the lives of these younger women. They seem unable to delay gratification and their track to success is quite fast. This group has little concept of earning their possessions—cars, homes, designer clothing—but feel entitled to it all. This belief system has been reinforced by family, media and society. An example is a young child/woman who has a VCR, camcorder, cellular phone, and her own computer. Soon enough she will have her own car and from there she may very well turn to drugs, alcohol, sex, and deviant behavior such as crime to get a charge out of life. These are the dangers for young women today, dangers that we did not contend with to the same degree twenty or thirty years ago.

In their own way, both younger women and babyboomers are searching for something meaningful in their lives, in a society ruled by sex, power, money, relationships, and appearances. As women awake and reclaim themselves, there is the possibility of inner peace, and a higher power in life, a spiritual nourishment. It is this opportunity that will eventually change the lives of women and offer them the right choices.

Introduction

Despite how far women have come in their lives, despite the persistent quest for recognition, women remain misunderstood. We are still considered *less* instead of different, and much of our lives is motivated by fantasies, while many of the decisions we make are based on illusions and incessant hope. It isn't that we determine to lead our lives in a distracted, doubtful manner—as many of us, in fact, do. Rather, our lives are handed to us while we stay immersed in the dream, the belief, the picture which was handed us by our parents and encouraged by our culture. As time passes, women grow disenchanted, even harmed by the illusion, but they cling to it all the same. It is only later that we begin to question our lives and are no longer detached from ourselves. Instead we become acutely aware of our choices or lack thereof, and at this juncture we begin to reinvent and reclaim ourselves.

This pattern of "detachment" in one's own life begins early in the development of a female. Social influences and expectations begin almost at birth and the messages are confusing. Sociologists agree that the past thirty years have produced major changes in the expectations and opportunities for women, and we have made great strides. Nonetheless, the messages are mixed for women, as we move on in the various realms of our lives. For every step forward, there is an obstacle, and we are unprepared and uneducated. While it might seem as if we were not paying attention—as if we have been absent intentionally—it is not always so. Not in the beginning.

Inertia seems to overtake many women at specific stages of their lives. The dictionary defines inertia as a state devoid of active properties, lacking the independent power to move or resist applied force. This inertia is a defense against the unknown and against life's disappointments. This may apply to one aspect of our lives—perhaps with our schooling, friendships, or with our siblings when we are younger. Later we use this "detaching" technique as a device to endure the adult phases of our lives. This inertia or detachment for women becomes a coping mechanism for what is otherwise unacceptable. Not always are consequences so dire or reactions so extreme that the separating mechanism is complete. Instead, we might be partially inert or partially separate from ourselves. For instance, our marriage may be strong, but our careers are intolerable. Or our careers may be rewarding but our marriage is lacking on an emotional or physical plane.

A bleak example can be seen in the popular 1991 film, *Thelma and Louise,* starring Susan Sarandon and Geena Davis. When Thelma (Davis) and Louise (Sarandon) embark on a weekend away together, unexpected events force both women to transform themselves. In the meantime the stakes become high and they get in trouble with the law. Shaking off their inertia has a profound effect, and while it is liberating, it is also tragic. In rediscovering themselves, the two women choose death over life.

Our goal, on the other hand, is to be prepared for a whole life, not a deliberate death from lack of choice. A more positive evolution of a woman who rediscovers herself can be seen in the classic film *An Unmarried Woman*, starring Jill Clayburgh. When the character portrayed by Clayburgh is unexpectedly ditched by her husband, she goes from being desperate because of the abandonment to reinventing herself. Her newfound independence is so complete that when she meets a man, she does not necessarily have to have him. She comes to see that in having her whole self, anything is possible.

Throughout the ages, women have been ill-prepared for life's challenges even as we have been instructed to adapt ourselves to the external world. With such a conflicting message, our progress has been slow and our self-recognition stymied. Over the last eighty years women have achieved the right to vote, yet in our country at present we have only two women on the Supreme Court, ten female senators, and four female governors. Only 22 percent of women in America graduate from college. However, the mean age when women marry has reached 27 while as little as fifty years ago it was 22.

These are real, if measured, achievements for women. The concern is for those women who do not succeed, whose plans and dreams go awry. Unless they realize that their life is less than optimal, they will not be able to begin anew. For these women, poor choices and decisions persist. The manner in which women marry and divorce exemplifies our recurring patterns, since in this area we tend to make the same mistake more than once. The divorce rate is over 50 percent in this country according to the U.S. Census Bureau, and the rate of remarriage among the divorced population is at 75 percent. The U.S. Census Bureau also reports that a first marriage fails after eleven years and a second marriage after seven years. Women who find themselves divorced for a second time exemplify a trend; they have not broken free of their past. Since they have failed to transform themselves, their standards remain the same.

Today, the number of working women is greater than ever before. Seventeen million single women are in the work force, including those who are divorced and widowed, and those who never married. Thirty-three million of this population are married women. The question is, who among this population of women is content with her personal life and leads a balanced existence?

Like Aurora, the Sleeping Beauty of the fairy tale, women are born with a childlike innocence, and our environment—teachers, counselors, friends and parents, as well as society at large—shape us. We are, in an ideal situation, nurtured when young but also acutely aware of the risks and deceptions in life. What often happens instead is that we are raised exactly as Aurora was, to be protected and loved. But when Aurora was put under an evil spell by a bad fairy, she was never told about it. In order to protect her, her parents did not inform her of the spinning wheel; she was not trusted with the information. Instead they banished all spinning wheels from the kingdom. Had she been warned of the spinning wheel, she might have avoided it, and then would have been empowered. Instead, her naivete led her to submission, and she was tricked into touching the spinning wheel, which she knew nothing about. She fell into a deep sleep that affected all her kingdom. In her sleep she waited for a prince to wake her back to life. The question left unanswered when the prince arrives and the fairy tale ends is: Does she fall asleep again to subsist, or is she awake—introspective and fulfilled?

Many of us are detached from our most precious days in various aspects of our lives. As my interviewees present it, this is a passive choice. For example, when women mother their children and they are small, they face an overwhelming responsibility and an all-encompassing devotion. The mothering is so demanding—combined with the demands placed upon a working mother, having a traveling husband or absent father—that women disconnect, depending on where they have been until now. There are women who see this as mere survival. "I recognized how trapped I was too soon," Angela tells us, "and I paid for it in a big way. Had I just waited until my kids were older and healthy, all grown up, I would have done better. It's one thing to be out of body, it is better than to be miserably aware of your set-up without any recourse. If you have choices, then reinventing yourself is paramount."

In contrast to Angela, Holly has made other sacrifices. "I have been out of touch when it comes to relationships with men since I was in high school. But I have always been aware of my own ambitions. I have wanted to be a performer since I was about three years old. And this is something I have achieved, with lots of ups and downs. In this area of my life, nothing stopped me. That is why I know how out of touch I've been in other areas—I can compare myself."

As with my other books, in writing *Reclaiming Ourselves: How Women Dispel a Legacy of Bad Choices*, I have delved into the lives of women by conducting personal interviews with a diverse group: over 100 women between the ages of thirty and the mid-fifties, of all ethnicities and social strata, from different parts of the country. I have combined this investigation with the opinions of professionals, psychologists, sociologists, and the thoughts of other writers. What has emerged is a recurring theme of reclamation as it pertains to women. Perhaps it takes a personal epiphany: a family member becomes ill or dies, a divorce takes place, a friend or family member moves across the country. Women transform themselves in their careers, finances, family connections, marriage, mothering, affairs, and remarriage. It is only if we can find a different, healthier path that we recover ourselves. Thus, these issues constitute the chapters of this book, which is in part an exploration of this pattern of evasion so prevalent among women, in part a guidebook, intended to improve our condition and pave our own way.

The world of the inert is divided into two categories. There are those who use their inertia as a means to dull the pain, helped by vices and defenses such as sleeping, drugs, alcohol, food, workaholism, love affairs or other relationships. Because it requires great energy and courage to change one's path and let go of the paralysis, we sometimes remain inert instead, although it is not in our best interest. Women who are unable to move forward, to leave their unsuccessful path, keep making mistakes and selecting unwisely. Another common theme is that of the woman who is bombarded and cannot deal with her situation. For instance, a woman who is immersed in an unhappy marriage or oppressed by caring for a chronically ill parent will use her inertia as a support mechanism. In both cases, women are so busy attempting to make a situation work that they cannot readily see what has true worth or lack of worth. When they do, they may still ignore this awareness in order to survive.

At the birth of the 21st century, we continue to live in a patriarchy. There are those scholars who believe this is a glib analysis—that the idea of a patriarchy is too large and vague to explain specific ills and triumphs. The fact is, however, that every step of our lives is taken in this patriarchy, and the effect of our actions is a result of the patriarchy's cultural values. So while women have undeniably gained power, men have sustained and increased their power, and remain more influential. Anytime that a woman achieves the upper hand in an aspect of her life it is a notable victory. In singular ways, women are on a journey similar to that in the past. In this journey, the old belief system holds fast. The inferiority these beliefs instill continues to dominate us. This is combined, in a contradictory way, with the new social pressures and media hype for women. The combination is dangerous and contributes to the chaos.

From innocent childhood, as described by William Wordsworth in his poem "Ode: Intimations of Immortality from Recollections of Early Childhood," we are thrown into adulthood and deprived of our early visions.

> There was a time when meadow, grove, and stream,
> The earth, and every common sight,
> To me did seem
> Appareled in celestial light,
> The glory and the freshness of a dream.
> It is not now as it hath been of yore:
> Turn wheresoever I may,
> By night or day,
> The things which I have seen I now can see no more.

There are cultural and historical influences from birth that restrict and ultimately discourage women. If they do not challenge the boundaries, they implicitly accept them. In order to accept them, they need to distance themselves. The most insidious distancing is one where we grow out of touch with ourselves; we go through the motions, but devoid of feeling. Or we feel what we are raised to feel, not what we really believe in our hearts. We are operating at a minimally functioning level. If we dare to dream, we don't remember the important dreams. Every day we live this life represents a kind of pretending, of getting through, of compromising. Eventually our real dreams fade, and hopes disappear. They are replaced with false hope, false love, a false existence. The most frightening part is that we barely know it.

The woman who loses her way is like Dorothy in *The Wizard of Oz*. There are those men, the Tin Man, The Cowardly Lion, and the Scarecrow, who travel with her to Oz. Each man serves a specific function for her—which is refreshing, since in real life women usually serve as functionaries for men. But ultimately it is up to Dorothy to get herself home, although she is surrounded by her "protectors." The moral of the tale is that Dorothy always had the power and the fortitude to go it alone. Not only she did not believe in herself, she did not recognize her own strength. It was the wrenching realization that the Wizard was a fraud and mortal man who could not help her that forced her to confront her own power. This is Dorothy's personal epiphany. Fortunately for her, it is learned early on in life, and she can avoid mistakes she would have made had she not been to Oz and back.

An epiphany such as Dorothy's may take years to occur. But once it does, the good news is there is the opportunity to live the rest of one's life in an enlightened state. Until this personal watershed and consequent reformation, women remain misguided, while steeped in responsibility and obligation. Then suddenly something happens, perhaps after many years: the loss of a loved one, a financial reversal, a serious illness, a divorce. Out of the revelation comes the solution, an understanding of who we really are. Only then is there the possibility of living a whole life, rich with those challenges and rewards that come to those who participate fully. Only then do we reclaim ourselves and become fully awake and responsible. Our first priority is that we not make the same mistakes again. With great fortitude and a belief in ourselves we strive to break the pattern of the past and build a promising future.

1

The Princess Falls Asleep

"We were never told anything growing up, and that is what harmed me in my adult life," Miranda at 35 tells us. "My sisters and I thought we were royalty and that we could have whatever we wanted. The expectations were clear—we were each to marry a prince and to live happily ever after. The husband would provide for his wife and while it would be romantic, more importantly it would be safe. In other words, there was no room for divorce or failed relationships in the picture—there was no room for unhappiness of any kind. If somehow we did not succeed, it was our fault.

"I worked very hard at getting married young to a professional man. This pleased my parents and won my sisters' approval. While I might have been deluded at home in my parents' house, it was worse in the marriage. I thought he was going to sweep me off my feet and that I would, figuratively, live in a castle. That was not my life, not at all. I was so young and so naive. I think I fell deeper into sleep at that point. What else could I do?"

SLEEP AS A COPING MECHANISM

Chasing an illusion is hard work. When women find themselves in the wrong life, the disappointment can be overwhelming. At this point, they may decide to fall asleep to get through.

As Annie sees it, at the age of 48, she has been asleep since her seventeenth birthday. "I was very immature and think that this is a reflection of how I was raised. The only negative part of my childhood was an atypical family love. My mother was not demonstrative; she had no experience of it from her own upbringing. I think today she feels guilty for not having been the best mother, but she knew no way of creating a loving environment for us.

"It was a totally female household with our father absent emotionally and physically. I was the second oldest of three sisters. We were never warned or told that the world was filled with evil people as well good. My mother did the best she could. I realize now that she was sleepwalking herself. That's why my sisters and I have been sleepwalkers for most of our lives. My sisters and I have spent most of our adult lives trying to please others."

Women try to meet other people's expectations to the detriment of their own self and their own needs. The axiom of women as nurturers and men as warriors persists with little revision. The myth of a woman as intrinsically in need of being saved endures and women are encouraged to believe that, whatever inner power they have, they never really own it. Women have not been trained or conditioned to do it solo. As psychotherapist Brenda Szulman, puts it, "We proceed to fulfill our unfulfilling prophecy. We don't really believe we can have it all without a man." Since the age of chivalry, women have denied their own needs in order to facilitate relationships that were valued and located at the center of society at that time. When a woman or "princess" finds herself with the wrong person, or in a completely unsatisfying life (which may mean living in the wrong part of the country, or being with the wrong group of people), one survival technique is to fall into a deep sleep.

This predisposition to fall asleep occurs in the lives of women because it is culturally driven. In a message that begins early in our lives and supersedes race and religion, women are led to believe that they are protected and pure. Simultaneously, we are burdened with expectations and complications. We are expected to be the good girl, the wife, mother, sister, friend, and confidante, although the recipients of our outlay of energy may not reciprocate. Then we become depleted and insecure. Sleeping or existing in a forgetful state becomes a way to contend with a life that astonishes and overpowers us. Initially, this eases the anguish and provides an escape. The sleep, or inertia, begins in our early teens and could last a lifetime, ebbing and flowing to different degrees.

IN AND OUT OF SLEEP

- **Women/Princesses may fall asleep long before adulthood**
- **Women employ this mechanism whenever the situation demands it**
- **Social expectations perpetuate the need to sleep**

Today, more than ever, media influences are overpowering. An example of this is the ultimate princess, the late Princess Diana, who was both victim and product of the media. A postmodern icon for her public, Diana was described by the former Archbishop of Canterbury as a "false goddess with loose morals." At the same time she can be regarded as a poor, abandoned princess. In this latter capacity, she resorted to James Hewitt as a lover, hoping this would ease her pain, and requested a divorce from Charles. It seems that in her sleep Diana remained married to Prince Charles, and in her wakefulness was strong enough to seek divorce. But it can be debated whether that was really the case. Either Diana was on her way to a new life when she died tragically in September of 1997, or she was stymied emotionally and unable to transcend the past. Was she a princess who awoke briefly to divorce only to fall asleep again in her choice of men and lifestyle—or had she really evolved?

There are other "princesses" in real life and in literature whose cases come to mind. Princess Grace of Monaco, who was also killed in a car accident, was very guarded in terms of her private life. Although Princess Grace projected a glamorous image to the world, we cannot help but wonder what her existence was like in the shoes of a real-life princess. She was unable to conceal the distress her spoiled children caused her. Her death brought to a head questions of what her life had truly been, and what her sacrifices and her unfinished dreams were like.

Queen Noor, the recent widow of King Hussain of Jordan, was also born American, as Elizabeth Hallajaby. She left behind her identity as a modern-day American woman for the fairy-tale existence of a princess—in fact, a queen. For the millions of women who are intrigued with any news of these royal women, there is an underlying sense that they sacrificed something of themselves in making their choices. The recurrent question is, were they fully awake in living the life of an actual princess, or is it necessary to sleepwalk, even in those gilded slippers?

In his exploration of the Kennedy women (perhaps the closest thing America has to royalty), *Jackie Ethel Joan: Women of Camelot*, J. Randy Taraborrelli presents Joan Kennedy as the least aware of the three sisters-in-law. When Joan and Ted were engaged, she sensed that Ted Kennedy was something less than attentive. Her mother Ginny told her, "He may be a little raw, but Ted can finance a marriage and a girl needs a man who can do just that. Keep him happy whatever you do." Taraborrelli quotes Joan as saying in retrospect, "I had no idea what I was getting into. I was just a nice young girl marrying a nice young man." Twenty-four years later Joan Kennedy could no longer tolerate her life and marriage. She was divorced from Ted Kennedy in 1982. For Joan, who had gone directly from her college graduation to her wedding, there was a gradual awakening, culminating in this result.

In everyday life with ordinary "princesses," women are reactive instead of proactive, accommodating others instead of themselves. "Without understanding themselves, women are nurturers," says Doctor Michaele Goodman. "These women wake up late in their lives or in their marriages and question what they are doing and how can they break free. This is very exciting for a therapist to observe. The key issue is why women do what they do. The answer centers around fears of abandonment and the need to be loved."

ABANDONMENT ISSUES

Women are pleasers because they are afraid of being abandoned if they are not. Losing status—be it marital, financial, or social—affects how they conduct themselves.

"I think I'm just waking up and I am 46 years old," Danielle says ruefully. "I've probably been sleeping since my twenties. Instead of making choices for myself, I've been involved with the wrong people. I've gone along for a good time without having very high standards for those who were my friends and in relationships with men. Although I have been surrounded by powerful people in the workplace, I did not realize the power they had. If I had been paying attention to the fact that they were wealthy people who really wanted to help me, I could have utilized the friendships for work and to meet people. These friends would have helped me, but I didn't know how much, nor did I recognize their positions.

"I think I have been unaware because so many negative things happened in my life and I never developed the skills to break free of bad patterns. I began my own business fifteen years ago, which is how I met these people. Although the business was very successful, I sold it because I was not in touch with myself enough and I let it go. I did not want to be responsible for employees and for other people's lives. I wanted to be invisible because I was so tired. Nobody told me that you have to look at the big picture. I wasn't told that when a business is no longer fun or creative and that it's only lucrative, that that's the real world."

It is a struggle for women to break patterns because they are so influenced by family and society. In order to wake up a woman needs a very strong image of herself. While she may not have someone waiting in the wings when she leaves a bad marriage, or a new job lined up when she leaves an old one, she must have some image in her mind that compels her to awaken and remain awake. Unless a woman can envisage what comes next, and how to get from one point to another with emotional and financial resources intact, she will repeatedly fall back to sleep. It is only if she has access to these resources that she will not retreat to sleep in the hope that her predicament will disappear. The personal epiphany occurs when a woman's life becomes unbearable. Then she will wake up at all costs.

Both famous women and unknown women have made poor choices in marriage and partnering for decades. With the divorce rate at over 50 percent, and the rate of remarriage at 75 percent, a woman need no longer feel like a failure when her marriage falls apart. She can learn what was lacking in the marriage, and become conscious of her needs. If women can establish a healthy existence for themselves, be it in remarriage or as single women, they have made great strides. As Katherine Rabinowitz, psychotherapist, says, "The poor choices women make in marriage are greatly influenced and modified by one's family history. There can be no doubt that it is the parent or parents who have the deepest and most lasting influence. Yet we also grow up influenced by peers, teachers, clergy and the general environment. As adults on an unconscious, completely illogical level, we want to right the wrongs of our past. We set up this scenario without realizing it by choosing partners who reflect our unhappy past, hoping this past can now be fixed in the present."

RECOGNIZING THE PAST

- **Women who are not in touch with themselves choose inappropriate partners**
- **Women who are not in touch with themselves misunderstand their needs**
- **Women who are not in touch with themselves misunderstand their partners**

"My only message from my mother was to escape her,"Talia, at 45, admits. "She could not manage her own life and she was out of control from the time I was small. She had big issues with my father who viewed her as irresponsible and demanding. She taught me what not to be, but I also realize she was a product of her time. Other families in the South were like that growing up. I had girlfriends whose mothers did not even own a checkbook.

"I think I became confused early on in my life because my parents gave me little direction. I was taught to work hard and was expected to support myself, and at the same time marry and have children. I feel I raised myself while my parents gave me material things, like an education, meals, a home. I ended up being overly responsible and not demanding enough. But I also became naive, which my mother also was on some level. It took me years to find my way. Even though I knew I could get along on my own and that I am a very independent person, I found myself in a relationship where I was dependent. I suppose I still wasn't watching out for myself at that point. I had no real sense of how to conduct my life and then I became a single mother and I raised my children alone. My husband had been so absent it almost didn't matter that we were divorced. But it made me take a good look at my life and what I want for the second half. I became involved in groups and took a part-time job. I began to be myself again. For that I am very grateful."

Approaching 35 was what precipitated a personal transformation for Grace, who believes that she was not a participant in her own life since she was in junior high school. "On the night of my thirty-fifth birthday," Grace tells us, "I realized that I wanted to have a child. I had been with a man who refused for four years to marry me. As I began to get stronger, I realized that he was asleep too, and that together we were almost co-dependents. I began to feel trapped with him because my needs weren't being met. For the four years that we were together, when I would demand more, he would make false promises, and I would wait. During the wait, I would become discouraged and I'd go back to sleep.

"Then this baby thing came up and I couldn't fake it any more, it was too important to me. I had never understood how to deal with men, even my male friends were treated differently by me than my female friends. If I had a girlfriend who wasn't fair about something, I didn't believe she was really my friend. When a male friend did something wrong, I should not have accepted it either. But there were fewer expectations with male friends, that was how I'd been raised or something I'd picked up just by living as a single woman. So when I stopped looking the other way with my live-in partner, I stopped looking the other way with regard to friendships too. I sort of cleaned my closet. I saw that I was with a man who did not want the same things I wanted. What I need from him compared to what I can have is a dream. And I'm very angry with him. It's made me take stock of my life. I have to have a child and raise one, one way or another. On this point no one will get in my way. I am finally getting my life in order."

Co-dependency, which Grace describes in her interview, is a source of dysfunction in today's world of relationships. For women who are co-dependents, it also functions as a form of sleepwalking. A woman becomes co-dependent because she has a poor sense of herself. She then loses herself in the relationship she has with a man. It requires great strength and conviction to stop this behavior and to form healthy connections. "Co-dependency," explains Dr. Michele Kasson, "occurs when a person fulfills a need by taking care of someone else. The co-dependent's needs are subsumed under the partner's needs. It is very difficult to break this pattern." Co-dependence is usually rooted in a long-standing family history and women tend to remain unaware of their habit because it is so entrenched. A cataclysmic personal event, such as a divorce or death or grave illness often precipitates a shift in the situation.

CO-DEPENDENTS BREAK OUT

After a family history of co-dependency, a life-altering event will break the pattern. Suddenly a woman is no longer lost and submerged in the relationship.

Women, in recognizing their own requirements, are becoming angry at their partners. The anger is a by-product of a failed relationship and a dissatisfying connection. Anger actually works in a woman's favor when she is modifying her life, while bitterness inhibits her ability to break free. As Shere Hite reports in her book *Women and Love*, 81 percent of the women she surveyed reported that their husbands and boyfriends acted "beleaguered" if a woman exhibited her anger. It is the gendered, cultural expectation of women to nurture and be emotionally supportive, without getting enough back in many cases, and without the chance to express themselves. Harriet G. Lerner observes in her book, *Dance of Anger*, that women who display their anger toward their partners without any positive change in the relationship feel depressed and self-betrayed. In addition, these women are then viewed as complainers. It is when one is angry enough for this to trigger action that it is effective.

ANGER AS A TOOL

- **Women are raised not to be angry**
- **Depression and disappointment are acceptable conditions**
- **It may take years for a woman to realize her anger**
- **Anger can provoke change**

Although women are raised to avoid conflict and to be dependent on their partners, Hite's survey also revealed that 87 percent of the women felt their partners were more emotionally dependent on them than they were on their partners. This defies what women are led to believe. Instead we are taught to think we are dependent on men for our well-being, and incomplete without them. In so many cases, it is only after numerous failed relationships that women open their eyes and understand what they can and cannot abide.

The double message for women is that they are to be attractive, seductive, and still good girls. They are to be working women and yet available to their husbands at the same time. Ninety percent of working women are doing traditional tasks at home, despite their long hours at work. Gerda Lerner, author of *The Creation of Feminist Consciousness*, reminds us that those women who are "victimized by the patriarchy" have also perpetuated it. The progress among our own daughters and women who have come of age in the past ten or fifteen years is striking. These women do not have the same expectations of being taken care of, and view marriage more as a partnership free of hierarchy. Their conditioning is not like ours and self-sacrifice seems less a part of the equation. That is not to say that these younger women do not hope to be with a man, but that their patterns are distinct from women ten or twenty years their senior. Women under the age of 30 are taught to go out and work and also encouraged to have a partner. The conventional path of marriage and family is the ideal. For a woman who remains single, she might have little choice but to support herself, as a course of survival. This woman is awake, but perhaps disappointed and still in pursuit of the dream.

MEDIA MYTHS

- **Women are sex symbols**
- **Beauty is power**
- **Youth and Beauty are the only values**

A recurrent message from the media is that women exist for love and marriage. The reality, as it emerged in researching this book, is that love-ever-after is one fantasy that women become lost in early in their lives. It can begin as soon as they have a high-school boyfriend, and culminate in a second divorce. As I wrote in my book, *The Men Out There: A Woman's Little Black Book*, women repeat their mistakes in the wrong partner until they are able to recognize their own needs and requirements. In the recent film *Nurse Betty*, starring Renee Zellwegger and Greg Kinnear, Zellwegger plays Betty, a nursing-school dropout from mid-America who watches her misogynist husband get murdered, then forgets about it, in what psychologists call "post-traumatic stress syndrome." Next she finds herself free to chase her fantasy, that of becoming a nurse to a soap-opera physician, on a show called "A Reason to Love." That Betty is in love with "Dr. David Ravell" and not the actor in the soap who plays Dr. Ravell, named George McCord (Greg Kinnear), is what drives the story. Betty is an adult Dorothy in search of the Wizard, a female unable to let go of the dream. The film invites us to wonder if Betty's amnesia is selective, a way to sustain her fantasy as well as a means of propelling her forward in her search.

The late psychologist Daniel J. Levinson wrote in his book *The Seasons of a Woman's Life* that women around the age of 30 are in transition, a time of child rearing and also a period when women began to face the disappointments in their lives. As he describes the thirties, it is a "structure-changing or transitional period [that] terminates the existing life structure and creates the possibility for a new one."

WOMEN IN TRANSITION

- **Women have babies**

- **Childbearing becomes their lives**
- **Disappointments become apparent**
- **Other possibilities present them-selves**

"I was told for years by my husband that I wasn't pretty enough," says Robin, who is 43 and has her own business today. "The irony is that when I married him he was thrilled to have a wife who he said was pretty and also intelligent. I had a job in public relations at the time and I was climbing the ladder quickly. I suppose I never really heard him because he made his intentions clear. I was the one who didn't hear what he said. He wanted a pretty wife to produce pretty children, and she was to be successful except he would not treat her quite as an equal. I realized many years later that he didn't care about me for who I was, but how it affected him. He wanted a family and he wanted good genes. Once I figured it out, I found this very calculating and it still disgusts me. My husband would tell me how to dress and what to do with my work. I had to look a certain way, and I complied. I kept waiting for his approval but it never came. Instead there was only criticism if I looked tired or pale or if he didn't like my outfit.

"He could not tell me that I wasn't smart enough so he would tell me what my work lacked or what I did wrong with a project. I kept acting like this wasn't happening. I kept pretending that this was just a quirk in his personality. Then as my daughters grew up, I saw that he did it to them too. He would break their spirit on their way out to a dance or a party, telling them their clothes weren't flattering or made them look a bit heavy. He was also very critical of their schoolwork. I saw all three girls in a positive light, in their schoolwork, and I thought they looked fabulous when they went out. I began to defend them, something I could never do for myself. At last I was really angry and I saw him as negative and nervy. I lost my respect for him and eventually I filed for divorce. My career was rocky for a few years, at the same time that my divorce was going through. But at least I saw my own worth, and that gave me strength."

MISOGYNY ALLOWED

- **Our culture has encouraged misogyny, which is an antipathy toward women**

- **Women as the second sex is an axiom of misogyny**

- **It has been a slow dawning for those women who leave misogynistic men**

It took Helene until her mid-thirties to admit that she felt trapped by the life she was leading. For five years she considered her options, and attempted to work on her marriage. Three years ago, at the age of 43, she divorced and began a new life.

"I am in the process of reinventing myself. Today I have more independence because my children are older and less dependent on me. I can admit that my marriage was a waste of the best years of my life, but I have my children–they are the product of this unsuccessful marriage. I have enjoyed raising them and I know they are my most valuable contribution to date. I say this although I practiced law for three years, then I opted to stay home with the children instead. I did not see this as a sacrifice because I was the enthusiastic mother and wife at the time.

"I look back on my marriage and I realize that I simply followed my husband around. Wherever he had to be for his career, I went along. He insisted that I take his name for his business when we were abroad and I did it. I did not want to take his name and I could feel myself hating it, but I did it. I was losing my identity and letting it happen as if I were powerless. Even before the children were born I couldn't practice law in the countries we lived. I know now that I was losing that part of me too, but there was little I could do. I was a fish out of water and unable to make it work.

"It has taken me years to feel that I can meet new challenges. I have fulfilled my childrearing responsibilities and I am ready to achieve something for myself. Had I had clearer goals for myself, I would not have ended up in this position, I suspect. I am happy to be divorced and I feel liberated in a way I have not felt since my early twenties."

In reading Helene's and similar stories, a common pattern emerges, that of women finding themselves in untenable situations and finally saying "enough." It is then that we make a conscious decision to either continue our sleep to survive or to resist at last, acknowledging that we lead a life that is unacceptable. It is apparent that many women who are cut off from a meaningful place in the world will fall asleep. When the world does not meet a woman's expectations, pretending or sleepwalking is an undeniable option. However, in this twilight world, there are few boundaries and no self-knowledge. In this condition, the woman or "princess" functions at a low level, and sacrifices herself. She takes her cues from the outside world because her inner self is being denied. It can take years to wake up, but when a woman does, she becomes empowered—prepared to revolutionize her life.

2

Early Myths and How We Lose Our Way

"I was not prepared for the world and came from a very sheltered environment, very protected," Julia explains. "My parents taught me nothing. Instead my sisters and I were raised to get through, but there were no conversations, no explanations. My mother never really respected our feelings and she did not teach us about what might come my way. No one told me that life is not fair and that it is a bad world in many ways. By the time we were adolescent, we understood we would each be married women one day, sooner not later. My mother's example was that if you give 90% to your marriage, you'd get 10% back. This example was so deeply impressed upon me that even after my first divorce, I remarried and found myself on the 10% side of that 90%–10% ratio again. But I was only thirty years old and I still believed in happily ever after.

"I cared very much what my family thought about my divorce and I saw myself as a failure. Maybe that is why I remarried again so quickly. No one in our family got divorced, and I was a major letdown. In this second marriage I was still anesthetized, but I was beginning to suffer symptoms of my unhappiness—it was the beginning of my self-awareness. Even in my drug-like stupor, I was beginning to sense that this life, this new marriage and all the pretense that came with it, was not for me. Of course, it took years after this realization for me to finally break through. Today, at 44, I feel I am finally on my way."

For those women who were raised to believe in the myth of happy ever after, it is particularly painful to realize that life is much more complicated than that, and that this kind of idealized happiness is elusive—if it exists at all. So much of our early illusions and understanding of how life should be come from our family environment, combined with social and cultural norms. And while each generation has its own aspirations and issues, for women who are in their late thirties, forties and early fifties, disillusionment with the "myth" of happy-ever-after can be quite intense.

While Mary Pipher, Ph.D. talks about girls raised in the 1990s in her book, *Reviving Ophelia*, describing these adolescents as "losing themselves," and crashing and burning "in a social and developmental Bermuda Triangle," it is also notable that women who are in their thirties (and were raised in the 1960s) also lost themselves along the way. Pipher sees a lack of "resiliency and optimism" in adolescent girls of today, who are coming of age in an entirely new world from what we knew. What we can relate to in these girls' experiences, despite the difference in how they express it (body piercing, drugs, early sex, etc.), is the misery with themselves. The irony is that for a large group who are mothers to these adolescent girls, the pain came much later—not in adolescence, but adulthood, maybe in midlife, and only after a life crisis or personal inspiration.

"My parents were depression children," Dolores begins. "And while they wanted me to be educated, they also wanted me to have a job that was practical. So they were liberated enough to want their daughters to work, and limited enough to ignore our talents. I wanted to be an artist, but my mother, who is also creative, sacrificed her calling to be scientific and told me to do the same. I have spent my whole life pursuing the wrong career because of the path my parents thought was best for me. Today I am a banker when I wanted to be a creative director. I see that I am doing well in a man's world, but still am frustrated. I am still not in the right place because choices are so limited for women. I was told to be a professional my entire childhood and I became a combination of someone who is both fearful and in need of short-term gratification.

"To the outside world I am a winner, a woman who has achieved a great deal. But I know what I have given up and why there was no real guidance from my mother. In the past few years I have been painfully aware of what I have missed. I believe that, had I done what I was truly good at, I would have made as much money as I do now.

"I blame myself for my cowardice and my parents for not understanding me better. I was constantly reminded that a liberal-arts education would be inadequate preparation in terms of the real world. Instead I became a banker, which is about as unartistic as one can get. After twenty-two years of this, a close friend became ill and I suddenly admitted how regretful I am about my work. Finally I was able to face my feelings and my mistakes. Now I am regretful twenty-four hours, seven days a week. My plan is that when my two daughters are in college and I've made enough money to retire, I will pursue an artistic career. Then maybe I'll feel secure enough and free enough to try."

In David Auburn's recent play, *Proof*, Mary Louise Parker plays Catherine, a 25-year-old woman who has no idea how to conduct her life. As the sole caregiver to her ill father, a professor and mathematical genius, she has sacrificed her own mathematical career and not even finished college. When Catherine's sister Claire comes home for their father's funeral, Catherine appears at a loss. It seems she never knew her way or recognized her own needs but was governed by the needs of others, primarily her famous father. While the audience is apt to pity Parker's character, by the end of the play her capability is recognized, complete with a gender spin so that she shows up her father's male student. It is fortunate for Catherine that she wakes up in her mid-twenties. There are plenty of woman closer to 40 or 50 who are positioned in the same way: as caregivers who are convinced of their ordinary capacities, not fully cognizant of their extraordinary gifts. These women have been asleep for twice as long.

The babyboomers–those women born before 1960–prove to be a population with the least direction and the most personal turmoil. For women born afterward, the choices have been more clearly defined and most aspects of their lives appear more integrated. The early myths die hard for these women who do not explore their capacities or respect their own desires. Partly this is because our families have such a great influence upon us. "Our parents are our teachers," Dr. Ronnie Burak explains. "Our perspective comes from our parents. The first eighteen years of a woman's life are spent with one's parents. And they give us a strong education on how we relate to the world. What happens with these women is that they then go out on their own and either choose someone who represents the same role models as their parents, or their opposite—which is another way of being controlled by them."

"I have remained idealistic," Beth admits, "because it was the only way to get through. I knew that my parents had problems and they fought. My father was out of work, which was a source of friction. Half of our family consisted of holocaust survivors and they were not a happy group. There was so much sadness everywhere that I had to retreat. I read a lot and tried to make life a fantasy. I pretended there was a pot of gold at the end of the rainbow although on some level I knew better. This way of dealing with things carried over to my adult life. I kept believing that everything was wonderful.

"I have made two mistakes in two marriages by pretending that things were not what they were. Only now, on the eve of my forty-third birthday, am I coming to grips with my failures. And yet my goals have not changed, only, hopefully, the ability to discern who will help me achieve them. I want to be secure, financially and emotionally. Over the years I convinced myself that I did not need money and that I could live on love. Had the relationships worked emotionally, who knows, this might have been the case. The truth is, I didn't feel safe as a child and I repeated that feeling because it was familiar, in both marriages, but in my second marriage to a greater degree. Today I am aware that I can start again, that it isn't too late. My idealism has faded recently and the reality has finally arrived. I'm not reborn yet, but I'm on my way. I am aware of why I've made such poor choices, out of stubbornness, to escape and because I wasn't in touch with my own needs. Instead I took care of those who gave very little back."

SOCIAL EXPECTATIONS

- **Women have more porous boundaries emotionally**

- **Male dominance is everywhere**

- **"Feminine behavior" is firmly entrenched in our culture**

"From the time I was three, I knew that my brothers would take over the family business and I would be excluded," says Kate, who is 46 years old. "And the strange thing is, I assumed this was acceptable. And although my parents did not send me to college for my MRS., like so many of my friends in the mid-seventies, their attitude toward my brothers confused me and made me feel inferior. The messages were mixed. They encouraged me to be whatever I wanted to be and then paid no attention to my achievements once I found my calling. There was this implicit message that I could be anything if I wanted to, and, of course, they wished me success. That was it, there was nothing beyond that, while my brothers took lessons in any sport that interested them—skiing, tennis, swimming. I wasn't exactly ignored, but forgotten on some level. And while I give my parents credit for not raising me to nab a man and marry him, I blame them for ignoring me. It took me years to figure this out."

Like Kate, Miriam, at 40, felt her talents never counted for much.

"Family life was so traditional that my brothers took turns feeding the dog and taking out the garbage, while I had to clear the table and do the dishes with my mother. When I married everyone seemed pleased, as if I had accomplished something. That was when I began to suspect that I had mis-understood, that this was all they really thought I could do. I was not only curious, but insulted by their behavior.

"Once I had children, I stopped working as a graphic de-signer and stayed at home with my children because my hus-band encouraged it. I felt left out of the world and I began to paint when the children were napping. After several years I showed my work to some galleries. It took two more years to sign with one. By then I knew not to look to my parents, my brothers or my husband for support. I resented their surprise—that I did it all myself and I have done well. My art has given me the confidence in other parts of my life. I tell my daughters to make sure they have something for themselves, and to create it, because nothing is given to women. I encourage them constantly because my mother simply put one foot in front of the other. Her job was to raise us and my personal talents had little to do with that."

In reading about Kate and Miriam's experiences, we realize that both families' messages were that daughters had fewer options than sons. Their parents did not believe that their daughters were as entitled as her brothers. Although it was an unfair treatment, it has affected both women's way of navigating their path. It has also, ironically, fortified their character and self-esteem. Apropos of how boys versus girls have been treated in our culture, a personal essay by the writer Alice Walker, "Beauty When the Other Dancer Is the Self," comes to mind. Walker writes of her place in the family vis-à-vis her brothers. When at the age of seven she is struck in the eye by one of her brothers playing with a BB gun, her brothers make her swear not to tell their parents. Walker, who is intimidated by this and respectful of her brothers' position in the family, acquiesces. Only when the seriousness of her injury becomes known does she reveal what actually happened. And years later it is one of her brothers who gets her to the proper doctor. But the lesson runs deep in Walker's essay—about family and betrayal, about inner beauty and the struggle women face daily in their lives to achieve, despite the limitations imposed upon us by gender.

"I look at my life as if it has been lived in two separate pieces," Natasha tells us. "The past represents my marriage, which might have been a fiction, but felt safe and right at the time. The present is my life as a divorced, single woman in a sea of single women. I think of my divorce as a death and because my entire life was spent coupled, I have trouble with my identity. My parents did not raise me to have a career, even when other girls were beginning to think that way. And while college was great fun, it wasn't a place where I felt I was noticed for my abilities. There was less encouragement for the girl students, or at least, that was my interpretation. I made the choice myself too, to not concern myself with a career. Instead I chose to be married. I went from my parent's home to my husband's home, much like my mother had done. Today I am unhappy because I was raised to believe in a life that doesn't exist.

"When I tell friends that I saw no issues in my marriage, I can sense their disbelief. They must have seen it very differently, but I was not ready to see it that way. What I think is that my husband was totally affectionate and loving and then he was gone and I feel totally abandoned. I know how ill-prepared I am for the world and I blame myself too, not just my parents or my former husband. Ultimately we have to take responsibility for ourselves. So many of my friends stopped working in the eighties to take care of their children, but they have gone back. I see that I am the one who can't get on with her life. I suppose I expected certain things at the next stage, once the boys were grown, and instead I found myself divorced. The promises made—by family and society—have not been realized."

Alongside the preconception that change is difficult and threatening is the awareness for women that we were not raised to take care of ourselves. This is a cultural issue, evidenced in

Natasha's interview, where she discusses how her parents allowed her to leave their home for her husband's home, without ever developing as a person with her own interests, talents, and abilities. In fact, she and an entire population of women were not taught to be independent, and lacked a personal direction as well. There is little self-fulfillment, self-confidence or self-esteem for this group of women. In order to revolutionize their lives, they must understand their own requirements and longings. This is the first step in an arduous process that begins in mid-life, instead of at birth, unfortunately.

There are women today who lead what was considered a traditional life and suddenly find it shattered due to the death of her husband, divorce, or simply the aging process. Her children grow up, she grows older, the children move out. If the woman has not developed her own skills, she now needs to reinvent herself in order to adjust and enjoy the rest of her life. Change is a process that we crave and fear, it is something we resist even as we most need it to go forward. A person has to have a strong desire to implement change in her life, because while the existence we know may be less than ideal, there is a familiar comfort in it all the same.

Leigh, whose husband died unexpectedly four years ago, has recreated herself out of necessity.

"I found myself alone after being part of a team for many years. Initially I was in shock and that lasted a very long time." Leigh pauses. "To lose a husband this way, so suddenly, makes you always question the loss. Like why did that have to happen? I do not wake up every day and say, how can I get through, but instead there is the disbelief that I am alone. I've been thrown into the role of a single parent to two young girls, and there is no one to help me out.

"I have always been a person who worked, but I threw myself back into it because there was no choice. The good news about being the only provider is that it has made me stronger. There was no luxury, no way to fall apart. I know that I have become a different person, that I am totally confident of my ability to take care of myself and of those who need me. I'm capable of doing everything and I do it alone. This is not like a divorce, or like being a single person without any children. I have stopped relying on other people because I have no choice. I know how unprepared I was for this role and how from childhood on I was expecting a happy, easy life, with kids and a husband. I see how far I've come. Being alone teaches you how not to be afraid. I miss my husband and I feel like I haven't seen him in a really long time. But I've had to accept that he will not walk through that door again. The biggest lesson for me is to never take anything for granted. I know how quickly it can be taken away from us—and I know how women are not ready for the tests of life."

SELF-ESTEEM AND CHOICES

The message that women are less comes from deep within the culture and is all-pervasive, covering all aspects of a woman's life. It begins in early childhood, is encouraged in educational environments, and lasts

into adulthood. This message causes women to underestimate themselves and consequently make wrong choices.

Jasmine, who has been divorced twice, realizes today that her marriages happened because her self-esteem was low.

"When I divorced the first time," Jasmine admits, "I felt like I had lost the best years of my life, like I had handed them to a man. That was what I was supposed to do according to my family—just not the divorce part. My first divorce was a shock to everyone. When I remarried, it was like replacing a dog in a pet store. The myth of marriage hadn't died, only my marriage had died. I have two daughters with my second husband and they are responsible for my waking up from a deep slumber. I began to question how I had been raised and how I wanted them to enter the world of people. Would they be prepared and ready for it, or would they be like me, and not know anything about life? As I grew stronger, my convictions of how to raise an independent girl became stronger. I had to face the mistakes I had made, to learn for myself and for my daughters' sake. This forced me to go back to what had happened in my own childhood.

"I realized that I had been overprotected emotionally and that until my daughters began kindergarten, I overprotected them emotionally on account of my pain. I also remained in a poor marriage because I had these children and that seemed enough for me. It took me a very long time to admit that I was prepared for very little when it came to emotions and coping.

Finally, I had no more excuses for putting my career aside and my marriage aside. What had been my purpose for so long, to raise my daughters, could not be my only purpose. It was a disservice to them and to myself. My obligation to them was not to burden them but to set them free. I had to begin again."

Notwithstanding inroads women have made in the patriarchy, the influences and anticipation of how women will lead their lives begins early on, and is encouraged by the convention-bound American family. Marriage has been held up to us as a cure-all for centuries. When children are born into the marriage, they become the focus, and in an unhappy marriage they may become a panacea for all the ills of the relationship between husband and wife. Margaret Mead, famed sociologist, writes in her book, *Male and Female*, that the "American family is oriented towards the future, towards what the children become, not towards the perpetuation of the past or the stabilization of the present."

Laura, who at the age of 42 is finally able to create the life she has wanted, was reluctant for years because of her upbringing. "Divorce was never a possibility, nor was being single for me. I am from a religious family and this was how we were raised. While I watched my mother's resentment toward my father grow, in every area of her life, I also saw her succumb. She had taken on my father's religion and while she resented him for that more than anything, she insisted that we follow the faith. I know my mother was comatose for most of her life, and that was how I knew I had to get out of my marriage. I felt that I would become her. And sometimes when I look at her now, I think to myself that when she is on her deathbed it will be heartbreaking to me because she has never lived. My mother's lack of options has impelled me to create options for myself.

"After being a stay-at-home mother for eighteen years in a perfect suburb with a perfect life, I knew I had to have something for myself. I stopped trying to make everyone else happy. I poured myself into my children to an extent and then I had to save a part of me. I could be called self-centered but it has also gotten me through. In my mid to late thirties, I woke up and asked myself if I could tolerate my poor marriage another minute. I asked my husband to pay attention to our marriage and he couldn't. For me, getting out of a poor marriage was what changed my life. I knew I wasn't satisfied and I knew I wanted more. I had become so damaged by my husband, who had never invested in the marriage but had invested in everything else. I was getting older and this forced me to do something."

The aging process can actually be a call to arms for women, a time when they take stock of what they did with the first part of their lives. In Laura's case, she was able to extricate herself from a poor marriage. This required her to go beyond her family's expectations and to break the rules. The conditioning of one's family has a profound effect upon us and it can take decades for a woman to realize this. As Joan Borysenko, Ph.D. writes in *A Woman's Book of Life: The Biology, Psychology, and Spirituality of the Feminine Life Cycle*, females learn early on, by adolescence, to hide their feelings behind "meaningless statements." "One of the unspoken rules of adult feminine behavior," writes Borysenko, "is that we must buffer strife, even at the expense of submerging our own feelings. When the adolescent learns this rule, she runs the risk of becoming a 'psychic sponge' for the negative emotions of family and friends."

"My mother raised me to think that I would marry a prince and be whisked off into the sunset," Angela tells us. "She never told me that relationships fail and that it can take years to meet the right man. I suppose that this upbringing prohibited me from having successful relationships. I kept buying into the bunk my mother had fed me and failing because the picture she described didn't exist. By the time I married, I was 39 years old. I married a man with a daughter, which was not the example set for me and clearly had complications. I understood that this child was part of the package.

"Tom, my husband, told me early on that he had to be with someone who would be good to Carly. He had a joint custody arrangement and Carly was only 7. I welcomed this relationship and it stirred emotions in me that I didn't know I had. This was a connection for me and I saw myself in a maternal role, which I liked. For the past six years, I have taken Carly everywhere and I have really enjoyed it. Being pulled in more directions because of her schedule combined with my own work schedule and obligations has been good for me. I honestly believe this relationship has been an awakening. I know that marriage to a man with a child and an ex-wife is not the 'dream,' not what I was taught to look for. But it works for me and has caused me to be in touch with a part of myself I didn't know."

Dispelling preconceived notions and expectations is one of the most difficult tasks for women. When it comes to marriage and children, there is an explicit message that this is the road to happiness. Although in recent years there has been an emphasis on developing other parts of our lives, marriage and motherhood are still held up as the supreme goals. The implicit message is that without a husband and, eventually, children, we are deficient. While this value system is still prevalent today, the received ideas and attitudes around women in our culture embraces are slowly evolving.

In *Women and Love: A Cultural Revolution in Progress*, author Shere Hite notes that while women view marriage as an emotional security, 18 percent of her interviewees between the ages of 30 and 50 state they do not want to be married. Forty-six percent of divorced women and 59 percent of widowed women do not want to be remarried—at least, not right away. Since women marry in response to a societal expectation combined with the desire for romantic love, there is bound to be disappointment. Often it is when a woman finds herself in a situation that is unanticipated and not what was held up as the norm—such as in Angela's case with a stepchild—that she discovers herself.

"Any kind of stimulus, positive or negative, can affect women," Brenda Szulman, psychotherapist, tells us. "Usually this happens because of an event, rather than a woman simply making a commitment to herself to change her life. When it is a positive catalyst, the life force becomes stronger immediately. When it is a negative catalyst, a woman might go through a period before she comes to the same heightened self-awareness."

NEGATIVE vs. POSITIVE STIMULI

- **Any significant loss can trigger a newfound declaration of self**

- **Any positive event can trigger a newfound declaration of self**

- **Either way, a woman becomes self-aware and begins to grow**

There are women in the public eye who exemplify triumph over adversity. In the recent senatorial election in New York, Hillary Rodham Clinton's victory over Rick Lazio seemed a personal reinvention for her. Only two years before, Senator Clinton had made the personal decision to defend her husband and to remain in the marriage during the excruciating Monica Lewinsky scandal. Once she put this behind her, Hillary Rodham Clinton determined to meet a political challenge, that of becoming a Senator in New York State. In an exhausting campaign, she covered every corner of the state. Her campaign as described by Elisabeth Bumiller in the New York Times was the "First Lady's Race for the Ages."

When mega-performer Tina Turner left her husband Ike Turner in 1978, there were those who questioned if she had enough power to perform on her own. Once Ms. Turner endeavored to go it alone, she recreated herself as a performer, becoming one of the most acclaimed female vocalists of all times. Cher, like Tina Turner, was brave enough to single-handedly turn herself into a rock star and actress after her divorce from Sony Bono in 1975. Another highly capable woman is Sally Field, who in the October 2000 issue of *MORE* Magazine, is described as having "charmed us on television and impressed the hell out of us on the big screen." Field's latest role is that of a movie director at the age of 53, thirty-four years after her debut on "Gidget." Each of these women deserve credit for their ability to assess their circumstances and to let go of what does not succeed in favor of what can. Whatever the motivation, it is the ability to shed the past and go forward with self-knowledge that is deserving of our emulation.

"I have become motivated to change because of a serious illness," Raine tells us. "While I am working on changing my life, it is a serious matter. It isn't as if I just cut my hair and became blonde. To me it is a more creative and a life-altering process. I am a computer analyst and I know that my work isn't satisfying enough. And yet, until I became very sick, I put all of my energy into it. I was taught that one should work hard and make a living. But recently I had to let go of this compulsion. I had to acknowledge that there is more to life than just working, which I might have known but never faced.

"I am not sure what I want, only that this illness has affected my entire life. I know now that I need to feel happy. Until now I was worried about making money and getting enough sleep at night. I always saw myself as having broken the mold by not marrying, but partnering, and by not having children. As long as I stood by my work ethic, I fit into a slice of society. I see that I don't want to fill that role. Eventually, once I get past the obstacle of my illness, hoping with drugs I can be cured, the threat of it will be behind me. But the lesson it has taught me will remain. I am now self-aware, in touch with my desire for an artistic outlet in my life. I would not have known this about myself, or faced it, if not for the illness. I would have kept making the same mistakes."

It might take the first half of a woman's projected life span to regain her belief in herself and to dispel the expectations of family and society, in whatever form they manifest themselves. Women have to be very motivated to transform themselves, because the alteration can be unpleasant and uncomfortable. As women mature and live through the events of life, they realize something is missing or lacking in their lives. Events that induce such feelings could be the severe illness or death of a parent or loved one, or seeing one's children grown and gone. Until then, a woman may be so absorbed in her day-to-day life that she doesn't always see herself—or hasn't the time and ability to change what she sees. At this particular stage of her life, this woman relies on whatever system she already has in place to support her.

FACING CHANGES

- **The unknown is always more threatening than the known**
- **Change requires a great deal of energy and inner strength**
- **Only dire circumstances can precipitate change**
- **Certain changes may feel like failure**

The fact that our society is not particularly reflective also affects women. In a world where outside forces seem larger than our inner voices and inclinations, women suffer more than men do. Because we are encouraged to live in a specific manner, anything else feels like less. What is missing for so many of us is a balance between the internal and external.

According to gender expert Nancy Chodorow, issues of dependency are not the same for men as for women. Chodorow views masculinity as a way of separating and femininity as a way of attaching. Women cannot separate easily, and the idea of it is fraught with fear and anxiety. Yet each voice in this book, each woman who has questioned the status quo of her life, or the influences and structures of her childhood, is moving, albeit at various speeds. A woman who breaks free of whatever has bound her is taking a huge leap into what appears to be the unknown. And yet there is gratification and fulfillment in taking this step, in facing what possibilities there are for each of us outside myth and tradition. This is, without question, the way we reclaim ourselves.

3

The Lull of Love and a Material World

"Most women my age are concerned about being in a relationship and eventually getting married," Caroline, who is 31, tells us. "I never thought about it in college like so many of my friends did, but now it seems to be a preoccupation. My friends who are single women are waiting to meet the right guy who will change their lives. It is definitely an issue. I see being in the right relationship as a natural progression to marriage. I want to have children and I want to be married.

"I have a good job but I've been at it a while. My view of it is that it is fine for right now. A year ago I saw it as an integral part of my career track but now it's just a stepping stone. I am looking to go further with it, but at the same time, my focus is on finding a partner. None of us talk about our careers as much as we talk about being with someone special."

Despite the high incidence of divorce (over 50 percent) in our society, most women still hold marriage in high regard.

Many interviewees told me that all their girlfriends are either married or hoping to get (re-)married. However compromised it might appear from the statistics—and from some of their stories—the institution of marriage persists as an ideal among the female population at large. The woman who rejects marriage either on principle or because of her own bad experience of it is the exception. If she has a take-it-or-leave-it attitude toward marriage, she may be more empowered because she has more choices. But the fact is that, for more women—especially those who are single in their thirties or forties—marriage looms large in their thoughts and preoccupations. (Their own mothers often "help" in this regard.)

If there is an obstacle to marriage for women today, it may be that they care about it too much. They still treasure it, but when they see their friends and family members' marriages founder, they hesitate, determined that for their part they are going to get it right. If they can't find the perfect soulmate of their dreams, they will continue to remain single. One consequence is that women are getting married at a later and later age. It's common for them to wait until they're in their thirties, and first-time marriages involving women in their forties are no longer rare.

Women who are ambivalent or uninterested in marriage are in the minority. A common trait among many of them is that they were disappointed in their fathers. They grew up witnessing the burden placed upon their mother and they identified with her. As a result, they shrink from the same situation—or the possibility of it—in a marriage of their own. Fathers who were alcoholic, or abusive, or unreliable breadwinners, or who fooled around, often spoil marriage for their daughters. It is not just fear of finding a similar mate; they remember how their mother was forced by patriarchy and social convention to remain submissive and continue to honor the husband as the man of the family. Daughters may identify with their mothers and feel humiliated on their behalf. Ultimately they lose some respect for both parents–and for marriage as an institution. They come to see it as degrading for the wife. But for women who had loving, reliable fathers, optimism about matrimony persists.

Love, by dictionary standards, is "a deep devotion or affection for another person or persons." As Michael S. Kimmel notes in his book, *The Gendered Society*, "Love has come to mean tenderness, powerlessness, and emotional expressiveness." Love, according to Kimmel, has also become "a woman's business, the home its domain." While the workplace forced men to be emotionless, his home and marriage were to offer him solace and be filled with shared feelings of love and caring. Our society greatly emphasizes romantic love, and marriage represents the culmination of that devotion and affection. All our lives, from childhood to early adolescence to adulthood, women are encouraged to cherish a man, to be awash in romantic love. Beyond social strata and cultural boundaries, there is the implicit expectation that each of us will fall in love, marry, and live happily ever after. It is this assumption, so ingrained in us, that often leads us astray, away from our own selves–lost in a fantasy of what love is meant to be.

LOVE OF RICHES

- **Women pretend to love a man for the lifestyle offered**
- **Our society has encouraged a co-mingling of wealth and partnering**
- **Women are motivated to find a successful man**

The lull of love and a material world blend together, and women continue to value lifestyle as much as love. For centuries, a lush life has been a motivation to "love" someone. When women settle or pretend, they may become immobilized and mesmerized by the media lure of a material life, which dulls other disappointments. Although women are more commonly represented as falling for a man with wealth, a man, too, can be impressed with a woman's earning power or inheritance. In either case, the idea of love becomes confused with the love of riches.

From my interviews a paradox emerges: marrying a wealthy man is a difficult endeavor. As part of the bargain they are expected to do a great deal in terms of sustaining the emotional life of the partnership. The husband is more likely to be consumed by his work, and less likely in terms of time and inclination to contribute to the emotional health of the marriage, and to the day-to-day running of the home and care of the children. Women who marry for money usually find themselves in a very traditional, old-fashioned role of wife/mother that is simply not satisfying for many women today. They see their friends educating themselves, and otherwise engaged in the world in ways that are personally empowering and fulfilling, but which are denied themselves because of the bargain they have struck—whether they were conscious of the implications of their choice at the time they married or not. This lack of empowerment can also make it harder for them to initiate divorce when they do become unsatisfied—and of course, the lure of material riches may persist, pulling them back into the marriage even as they have the itch to move out and move on.

Sam, 46, lives in a fashionable community north of L.A. "I was 22 when I married. Eliot is a very successful alpha male, an orthopedic surgeon. We met in college, and our relationship began as a very passionate affair. I was very much in love with him, and for the first few years of our marriage I was living the fairy tale. We had two daughters right after marriage, and I ran and still run what you might call a Martha Stewart household. Eliot was—still is—a stereotypical frat boy. We own a boat and every year he hires a crew and goes to Mexico to participate in these amateur regattas. I began to resent the time he spent away from me and the children, and I was feeling very alone in the marriage. I'm now totally out of love with the guy—I think he's superficial and never really grew up. For years I tried to get us to go to therapy together but he resisted—said he didn't have the time. I think he was intimidated by the idea.

"When I was 38 I started an affair with Donald, an old friend from college, a psychiatrist, also married, with three small children. In his own mind he justified the affair by thinking of me as an unconventional client, whose fantasy he was graciously fulfilling by giving me what I lacked with Eliot. Then he fell in love with me, and started being indiscreet, calling me at inappropriate times and so forth. Well, of course, Eliot found out and freaked. He began to terrorize me, waking me up in the middle of the night to demand sex, yelling, screaming and breaking things around the house. These episodes alternated with times when he would get very remorseful, saying how sorry he was he had neglected the children and me. From my perspective, it was too little too late.

"Now I'm in love with Donald, and I want to start a new life with him. But I'm hesitant. My daughters are emotionally fragile, and I fear the effect a divorce would have on them. I'm also very attached to the home I've created because of the time I've put into it. And I don't trust Donald to carry through with his own divorce even though he's said he'd do it if I do. The fact that he's waiting for me to make the first move concerns me; and I haven't been able to take that step. Now I'm in therapy–alone–hoping to come to some resolution while I'm still young enough to start over."

Women are not trained to believe they can have it all, and so they continue, on some level, to achieve vicariously through their husband's or their children's achievements. Women have traditionally empowered themselves through these channels. When a woman realizes the hollowness of this life that she has carved out for herself–the one she was convinced was the right path–she will reinvent herself. With enough initiative, this may result in a divorce, a new job or career, an effort to further her education, to renegotiate the marriage, leave the marriage, or find a new partner.

"My parents had a lousy marriage," says Jenna, who at 46 has left a 24-year-old marriage. "And I had no one to show me what to expect. But I sure knew that a man counted because my mother stayed with my father. That was the message—that she had to stay because women have to have men. Jack and I were so young when we married, it couldn't have been healthy for either of us. But his character is another story. For years I gave him more credit than he deserved—I thought I had no options. Only when it was so intolerable did I let it end. I saw how pathetic and selfish he was and I finally left. I had stayed for the comfort of it. It wasn't emotional comfort but material comfort. And financial. I came from a very poor family and he made a good living. This was important to me.

"The sad part is that he forced me into reality instead of my getting there on my own. I know now that he did more for me by ending it than by being with me. It was so painful to realize that for all these years I had been married to a man who was not who I thought he was. No wonder we kept fighting—he wasn't doing what he was supposed to be doing. He couldn't do it. I admit that credit cards and a pretty house and two dogs were my blindfold. When I was on my own I struggled and worked several jobs, but it made me stronger. And I began to know myself and what I would not do again."

The undying belief that material resources will bring joy and a solution to our problems underlies many a romance and marriage. Not only is this the case in the lives of a multitude of everyday women, it was also the motivation of the late Princess Diana in her marriage to Prince Charles. The lack of success in so visible and promising a story is a reminder of how profound the lull of love and a material world. As Simone Simmons describes Diana's plight in her book, *Diana: The Secret Years*, the princess was miserably married to Charles, without any support of the royal family. From the start of the courtship and marriage, any hope of true intimacy had been preempted by Charles' longstanding relationship with Camilla Parker Bowles. The material comforts of being a princess continued, however, a part of being a princess unaffected by Charles' infidelity. "Somehow she had forgotten that in the outside world people carried money in their pockets and purses as she had once done," writes Simmons. "Little things like that made me wonder what other aspects of reality had been siphoned away from her young understanding when, early in 1981, she began basic training as Princess of Wales."

MATERIAL WORLD / MATERIAL GIRL

- **The media emphasizes money and wealth**
- **The old adage "money can't buy happiness" is disputed**
- **We feel denied without the material goods**

"I see now how protected I was by a moneyed life," admits Rachel. "I lived in a gilded cage but I didn't know it. Here I was with people who had so much and were so impossible. This was an elite world and there was nothing real about it. It was a far cry from Middle America. My parents were very conservative and not interested in the kind of life I lived. Of course, they had their own set of rules and belonged to a country club. I felt like *Goodbye Columbus*, I felt like I was entitled to a similar life. Nothing could go wrong, because I was entitled. When my husband left, a person I had never really known or understood, the bubble burst. I was expecting a huge settlement, but the fact is, when you earn a lot of money, you live large, and you incur debts proportionally as large as couples with smaller means. That was an additional incentive to settle and remain in the marriage—in the bubble. But when the time came, I can honestly say there was a part of me that was not sad to see the bubble burst—I think the realization that it was all based on childish values and expectations made me ready for it to blow up."

PRINCESS IN TRAINING

- **Regardless of our lifestyle or culture, we continue to search for true love**

- **Regardless of our history—divorce, single motherhood—we continue to search for the prince**

- **Regardless of our culture, we tend to believe a man can save us**

Jamie, at 37, has decided not to seek a material life with her future partner. Instead she is looking for other qualities which have become important to her over the years. "I was married very young, which is a part of my culture, and I have been separated from my husband now for four years. I have three children who are grown up now. The marriage didn't work because when the children were young, I needed my husband to do better. I was madly in love with him but I also had this image of a picket fence, a house with a yard for the kids. He didn't want that kind of pressure and things changed. Throughout all this, I had a good job, but not a career. For me, family life was more important, and the job, with benefits, existed because we had to live. With three children, I wanted my husband to pitch in, and to make money for us to survive. I never needed a lavish life, but I wanted him to maintain us on some level.

"Life is very expensive and my husband disappointed me by not helping. I never expected things to go as they did. He is a good man with a good head on his shoulders, but he had no vision of the future. I wanted to advance us, I wanted us to move forward, and I wanted to move forward for myself. I told him I did not want to stay in a hole. I suppose I had misunderstood him, because our values were not the same. Unfortunately, the qualities I need in a man do not always come in one package. I basically woke up and decided I would take care of the kids and myself. I learned that there are many layers to a person and that what you see is not always what you get.

"I was not raised to believe that marriage was the answer

and my mother, who is not with my father, understood why I left. My judgment was that I would do better on my own and that I couldn't live with someone who couldn't meet me halfway. Today, because the kids are out of the house, I would consider having a relationship. It would be about honesty and civility, love and commitment. The money part doesn't count because I won't have children with this man. I can pay my own way, I just don't want to support anyone else."

This need that Colette Dowling uncovered in her book *The Cinderella Complex* is apparent in the lives women lead, and begins in childhood. It is then that a girl is taught that someone will be there, a protector and support system. This culminates in a sense of inferiority that plagues so many women. Dowling's definition of "The Cinderella Complex" is "a network of largely repressed attitudes and fears that keeps women in a kind of half-light, retreating from the full use of their minds and creativity. Like Cinderella, women today are still waiting for something external to transform their lives." So often this external something manifests in the form of a partner or husband. If a woman is in inner turmoil or not aware of her own self when she marries, she will hope to be cared for and unconditionally loved. No wonder the confusion is so profound for women, who have to discover on their own that partnering, deemed a solution for centuries, might itself be the problem.

Thus the dilemma. On the one hand, we have been encouraged to find a partner since time immemorial. But having lost ourselves along the way, we are ill-equipped to judge who the right partner is, and what balance works in the relationship.

GHOSTS OF CINDERELLA

- **In recent years women have strived to be independent**
- **Despite this journey, we are still looking for a protector in a mate**
- **The more we develop our own skills, the better equipped we are for the real world**

"I was raised with the myth of Prince Charming, who would take care of me in every way," explains Cameron, who at 43 is divorced and looking to meet someone in the near future. "This man would be everything and pay the bills. My role model was my father who was more successful than my mother. While my mother worked, my father was a professional, and made more money. Nothing was ever stipulated but I was always very realistic, I knew that I would have to be with someone who could take care of me on a certain level. I dated men who were not very eligible and I did not take them seriously. I was looking for a good husband, with future potential, and I knew I would not marry a carpenter.

"In the late fifties and sixties there was a certain ethic, that of the American Dream. Everything was joyous in suburbia, we were children being raised for a joyous adulthood. There were very few divorces and there was never a doubt in my mind that I would be married to a dream man. I had friends in college who were petrified that they would be old maids. I never worried. I assumed that I would marry a lawyer and that it would make me very secure, just as my mother had been very secure with my father, who is a lawyer. So I did just that and for years it was as I anticipated it would be, a blissful, superficial world. All hell broke lose when my husband wanted a divorce. Then I realized how little I knew about the world at large."

The October 2000 issue of *Elle* magazine published an article by Louisa Kamps entitled "The Pursuit of Happiness. It's Guaranteed in the Declaration of Independence—But Are Americans Too Hung Up on Bucks to Concentrate on Bliss?" Kamps acknowledges that money can buy happiness if someone is impoverished and needs a roof over their head. "Once those basic physiological requirements are fulfilled, however, you get less bang for the buck. Money doesn't have a lot of influence over the needs on the next plane of the pyramid: love and esteem," Kamps writes.

PLAY IT AGAIN

- **Women search for the same type of man their whole lives**
- **This type is often an unhealthy match**
- **If we can break free, we have the chance to get it right**

Even for those women damaged by a series of failed relationships or failed marriages—whether owing to an over-optimistic belief in the power of wealth, or for other reasons—

there is the enduring hope of getting it right the next time. Women have a tendency to endow a future partner with qualities that may not exist, and misinterpret who the person actually is. The fantasy is much improved over the reality. The model to emulate is the woman who breaks free of her repetition and finds herself satisfied with a different kind of man in a relationship that is unlike those of the past. In order to achieve this, we have to be in touch with our inner selves and our own needs. Only then can we have an understanding of what was wrong with the past.

Mary Ann Lamanna and Agnes Riedmann define three stages of mating in their book, *Marriages and Families.* The "stimulus stage" in dating involves physical attraction, the "values stage" is when the partners compare their individual values to see if they mesh. The final stage of mating is when the couple explores "role compatibility," which is when the partners navigate their roles in a potential marriage. After passing these tests, the couple may proceed to become engaged and married. What causes a cog in the works and a failed relationship down the road is when one of the partners is posturing, or what Lamanna and Riedmann call "imaging–projecting and maintaining a facade as a way of holding the other person's interest." When the honeymoon stage of a marriage has ended, the risk becomes that the person who was imaging is now revealed for who he or she really is. In many cases, the revelation is slow and may take years to develop completely. This is also because women invest so much in the hope of the success of the relationship. This brings us back to an ongoing theme–it is when we are in touch with ourselves that we begin to have clarity and the courage to face change.

"My problem is that I put my entire self into a relationship and I do not focus on my needs as much as the other person's," Adele explains. "I am 31 years old and I was married and divorced in my early twenties. That relationship failed because I was too young and didn't know what I wanted. Then I became involved very quickly with men after that. My biggest fear was being alone. I kept thinking the next guy would be right and I am only now learning that I can be okay without a man in my life.

"The past two relationships have taught me a lot. I have been with very narcissistic men and then I end up feeling alone. I was treated well and they both lived nicely and had great careers, but that didn't make them the answer. I look back at my ex-husband and I see that he was very kind and loving but misguided and lost. It was a co-dependent relationship and I have a tendency to go that route. Once I get into it, every second will be spent with my partner and there is no separate life. I have always looked for love, and so I might be in love with love and lifestyle. I see that I fall in love with the idea of a person. I even create the idea of what I want this person to be like and then he isn't like that at all. I have been so trained to be taken care of by a man that I can become blind to who that person is."

PERPETUAL SEARCH

Women of all ages with assorted

histories are looking for the answer in the next relationship.

vs.

KNOWING ONESELF

If women know they are worthy in their own right, they will not make the same mistakes again. This belief in oneself is essential to move forward.

For so many women, the wrong choice is made in a partner because their self-confidence is so impaired that they are unable to discriminate. In this case, a woman is prone to leave one partner and find another who is similar to the first. It is only when women have a strong sense of self that they will not repeat their history and can avoid future failures.

SELF-KNOWLEDGE AND CLARITY

- **We are not in touch with our own needs if we choose the wrong partner repeatedly**

- **Group therapy or intervention helps**

- **A crisis can be a wake-up call and change one's pattern**

"I am slow to realize," Dina, at 40, admits, "that I want someone to care for me. The first time I was married I was 23 and I thought it was the thing to do. My father and mother had been married forever and there had been an implicit expectation that I would go to college and then get married. I needed to do it for personal reasons–to anchor myself. I'd been so wild in college that I longed for the kind of peace and quiet that marriage represented. I didn't want to fool around anymore, but I wanted some stability. Then I was too anchored and I wanted my freedom. I had done the right thing: I had found a partner, had started a life and landed a good job. Everything was so stable that I felt trapped and bored to tears.

"It wasn't until my second marriage that I realized that I marry to avoid being alone, to be in a couples world, where everything appears safe and sound. I thought this second husband would be fun, while the first had not. I had missed having fun in the first marriage, which lasted nine years. So I was ready for some fun. There was excitement, definitely, and it was a walk on the wild side. It got out of control and I came to my senses. I'm not sure that having married the opposite of my first husband the second time was the answer. I wish I had found some kind of happy medium. But having felt so insecure for the past five years in the marriage, I am ready for stability again. I know now that wanting someone to love isn't enough. There have to be other parts that work. Lifestyle and financial security matter to me, because they were lacking both times. I am very tired of being the breadwinner. And I am very tired of fooling myself into thinking these men are more than they are. The funny part is, I'm not finished looking. I'm ready for a partner where the two of us fit, this time for the rest of my life."

Women often marry men who fill in the empty voids in themselves. An example of this is a wife who is well organized while her husband is disorganized. Or if a man is a free spirit, he will look to his partner to be grounded. Dr. Ronnie Burak tells us that while opposites attract initially, as time goes by, we want our partner to be more like we are. "What I see in marital counseling, " says Dr. Burak, "is that the very reason why someone picked her husband is now what drives her crazy. Women have to weigh the cost/benefit ratio but often it comes to a breaking point. What we need to remember is that no matter who we are with, we will discover their faults eventually."

FALSE LOVE

- **Women marry the wrong men**
- **Women are afraid to be alone**
- **Women pretend love is satisfactory when it inflicts pain**

In Cindy's case, no one could convince her to let go of a negative lover who was depleting her energy. "When I was 30, I was seeing a man who was poison. My family, who is loving and kind, could not persuade me to let it go, nor could my friends. When I did try to get away, I ended up in the hospital after a fight. Finally I listened to my family. I knew I had to move on. I woke up a little bit and admitted that it had been a very bad scene for me. But I certainly wasn't in charge of my life just because I'd left this man. Instead, I sort of wandered for years afterward. It took me a long time to figure out what I wanted. I had a few other bad relationships with men who lied and were not who they said they were.

"Today, at 44, I am a bit better, but it has been a long hard struggle. I am realizing that I am my own person and not just the person who people tell me I am or who they expect me to be. I am with a man today and it has been very rocky. He is not physically abusive but he can be cruel. I was desperate to marry him for a while, but not now. There are parts of him that I love and parts of him that worry me. I am asking myself some important questions, like is this man ready to be there for me? Can he give me what I need? I want someone to be there emotionally. I have been with this man for three years. Two years ago, I had to be married to him, had to have his child. It didn't happen but I stayed with him anyway. Now I am asking myself what I would do if I don't spend the rest of my life with him. I do know that jumping through hoops for him doesn't help either of us. I don't want to jump through hoops for any other man either. It has taken me years to understand that emotional abuse is like physical abuse."

Although we have the best intentions to have a healthy relationship, one in which the love is rich and rewarding, the rate of divorce, remarriage and second divorces stand testimony to repeated mistakes. Love relationships are at the very center of our lives, and hold out more promise than any other aspect of our existence. What is intriguing is how many women who have been interviewed lament their poor choice of partner, a subsequent break-up, and their inability to find the right partner afterward. The fear is that we grow older, without necessarily growing wiser. The goal is to become more in touch with our own needs and, with this maturity, find a partner who serves more than ego desires. The relationship works from the inside out, eliciting the best in both partners. This takes work, time, and self-actualization.

Socialization in the direction of reduced self-esteem begins early in a woman's life, and never lets up. As we saw, girls are encouraged to be conformists, compliant, "good girls." Attitudes pervasive in society mutually reflect and reinforce this message. Women tend to earn less money for equivalent types of work. It is part of being female in a patriarchal culture. Midlife is a dangerous time for the female self-image because it is challenged by many factors—loss of beauty, an empty nest, divorce perhaps, a feeling of being out of touch intellectually while having tending to the home, insecurity about one's marketing skills in today's high-tech world. But it is also a positive time for self-esteem because it is when women are emotionally and intellectually ready to take a step back and reflect critically on their own lives and the values that have shaped it. Building self-esteem requires a willingness to be alone for periods of solitude, to be reflective, to consider the strengths and weaknesses of themselves and others—to dare to be critical of things that they had always accepted uncritically. It requires a willingness to dream of new opportunities, some of which, including possible relationships, may have been staring them in the face a long time. Many women report getting help from private therapy at this stage of their lives.

Marriage unquestionably works better for women who have a realistic approach to the institution. But based on my pool of interviewees, there seems to be a lack of illumination for married women, especially in their first marriages, undertaken between the ages of 35 and 55. For those women who exist in this fantasy world that inevitably fails them, there is the necessity to sleepwalk as a survival mechanism. This avoidance technique keeps women from admitting that they feel ignored, mistreated, underrated, neglected and unappreciated in their marriages. When they do admit their feelings, the results vary. Some women confess they married for the wrong reasons, and take responsibility for their actions. Others feel they were forced into the marriage by influences such as family, society, or their partner's insistence. Others do something for themselves, such as go back to school or begin a new career. The marriage may end in divorce or be renegotiated. These personal epiphanies take years and are often triggered by circumstances such as an empty nest, when all the children have left the house, by a family member's death—which forces us to ask ourselves questions about the life we lead—or by a serious illness affecting either partner. Until then, women occupy themselves with the mundane—friends, work, family, the clutter of our everyday lives. They are unable to look at the fundamental issues and are too fearful of change and the implications of altering their reality, even if it is below the standard.

REALITY CHECK

- **Women in midlife are still in search of a fantasy life**
- **As the years go by, their search**

grows more desperate

• A reality check is in order

Uma has left a long-standing, disappointing relationship for "a better life." She feels that at the age of 39, she has many options. "I know that breaking up served a purpose, but so did the relationship. I should have listened to Paul in the beginning when he told me that he had a nervous breakdown when his last girlfriend left him. I should have suspected that he would use a similar technique on me if things didn't go well. And I knew that he had selective hearing, and was a kiss-and-make-it-better kind of person. With all these clues and my own instincts, I am so sorry that I stayed with him for some of the best years of my life.

"I thought that a comfortable relationship such as we had was the answer. And my career was so exciting and important for so long that I could only deal with a simple guy, someone who was laid-back. We had talked about getting married and he was not interested since he did not want children. I never wanted to have children either. All of my creativity went into my work. But I never stopped believing in love. And that is why Paul and I bought a house together, all the while knowing he was not enough for me. I stayed out of laziness and complacency, and because no one likes to be alone. Then he began to fall apart and couldn't handle any stress.

"Suddenly he wasn't gentle and had a lot of anger. He said I worked too much. That was when I realized he was right, I did work too much. And so I quit my job and left him at the same time. I felt the possibility of my life, I knew there was a wide world out there and I was finally ready. I will never compromise myself with someone again. I will never choose the wrong partner because it is so easy to fall in with someone. I have become more selfish and more self-aware. I am not even sure I will ever live with someone again."

LOVE AS THE ANSWER

- **The idealized person will make life perfect**
- **Without him, we are incomplete**
- **Everything else falls short of having the right partner**

vs.

OURSELVES AS THE ANSWER

- **No man is a prince/rescuer**
- **We become complete before we search for our "other half"**
- **Only when we know ourselves can we grow with someone else**

"Men always wanted to marry me," sighs Virginia, who at 40 found herself divorced, "but I resisted and did not marry until I was 34. I was totally unprepared for this marriage and totally unrealistic. I had a terrific man but I didn't know what commitment or compromise meant. I expected so much from him—all of my wishes, my dreams and desires were to be fulfilled by him. I didn't anticipate that he would have issues of his own, I just thought that he was there to care for me. I wanted it to be easy and effortless, and I had no idea what it takes for two people to work on a marriage.

"I grew up thinking I would have a big family and a house in the country. But until I was 34 I lived in a city and worked hard as a single woman. I wasn't committed enough to my dreams. I was so busy trying to build a life that I got off track— I thought that being a successful business woman mattered the most, that being an accomplished athlete was important. I suppose I was selfish because I had so many requirements, with my circle of friends, and family obligations to my sisters and brothers, and I became bogged down with all of it. I didn't even consider carefully that my husband would have been happy to start a family and to live that life. It's as though I didn't realize what he had to offer. He was a loving, competent, undeveloped person, who had worked his entire life. My father had been hardworking and driven, and I liked that. That was what I got. But he needed a makeover. Instead I threw in the towel. Somehow I was unprepared for the struggle. I see now that was totally unrealistic. I didn't understand what a man brings to the table.

"I think my divorce was a lesson about what love is and a lesson in who I am. I did not look at myself in the marriage, I was totally out of touch with reality. It is very sad because I cannot go back. I tried to patch it up after I had created such chaos and had broken his heart. As soon as I dated a bit, I knew I was wrong about my husband, about marriage and love. I asked my husband to give it another go around and he told me he did not want to try again."

The promising future with her husband which Virginia forfeited due to her own lack of self-awareness represents a less common situation than confronts those women who find themselves in the wrong relationships and stay. Women will marry a partner who they know in not right because they are afraid to be alone. Or they will find themselves in relationships where the dynamic is unhealthy. When women mistake false love for real love, loneliness and desperation are the result. These relationships are known as addictions. There is a lack of trust and a loss of control of our money, our heart, our mind and our best interests. It is a myth of romantic love that keeps women in these poor relationships for much too long.

"Several years after my separation," begins Lillian, who, at 34, is single, "I met someone who seemed to be the best thing that ever happened to me. We went through all the stages of a positive relationship together and it began to fail. I began to see that I had made the same mistake again, and that this relationship had some differences from my last and also was the same. The bottom line is that he let me down. I was looking for a provider and someone I could share my life with. I wanted stability but I also wanted love and honesty. And we had that, for a while. The problem here was that he was a womanizer and I was blind. I only saw what I wanted to see and then finally, I had to look at the truth.

"Today I am with a new partner. The heart is not all in it the third time around. I am very cautious. I am also listening better and waiting to see what happens. We've been together almost one year. After the last relationship, I realize that I wasn't prepared. So I took hold of myself and figured it out. I don't need anyone to pay my way, I am too independent for that. But I do need someone to care for me and to know my feelings. And I do not intend to pay for a man, or to support him, nor does he have to support me. When I consider living with this man, I take all this into account. I am looking for someone who is moral and responsible. That is what I have learned, someone I can meet in the middle."

Women, whether in their thirties, forties or fifties, do not give up hope of finding the right partner and starting again, or perhaps marrying for the first time later in life. The partner is to be a soulmate, someone who is supportive emotionally and in terms of goals and lifestyle. Many women complain that such a man is difficult to find, and that the "good men" are mostly married and unavailable. The concept of being alone in the world is still frightening, no matter how far we have come in terms of financial independence, and the idea of a devoted partner is held in the highest regard. For those women who have been disappointed and do not wish to remarry or recouple, underneath there is perhaps the secret hope that they will find happiness with a partner at last. But the frantic search for a man, the anxiety about missing the boat with regard to marriage/children/houses, is behind them, and is replaced by the thought of a lover, for the sake of the sheer joy it brings. These women can take care of themselves, and so the choice becomes theirs alone.

According to American Demographics, 88 percent of those

husbands in a successful second marriage say it is a happier union than their first marriage. For a woman who has never been married, there are the idealized hopes and dreams of any bride. For a woman who has been married before, there is a maturity that she brings to the relationship and a self-knowledge that she has gained through the difficulty of divorce. This woman is usually less conventional in her approach and less likely to think she has landed a man. It is ironic regardless of how far women have come on their own, in terms of independence, divorce and careers, that they continue to believe their future is settled and they are secure once they have married. Many men still believe, as stereotypical as it is, that they have been reeled in and are now frustrated by marriage with its many demands and responsibilities. These attitudes have not changed, no matter how far we have come, and the motivation for many women to marry continues to be safety and security.

The results of several studies make a woman's standard attitude to marriage all the more curious. Jessie Bernard's study conducted in the 1970s indicated that men, not women, benefit most from marriage. More recently, we have learned that men over 40 fare much better health-wise when they are married, since they are happier when married and less depressed, while unmarried women are actually happier than married women. For women "waking up" from the dream, there is the possibility of approaching marriage in a new way, one that will meet their needs better. It involves less of the romantic myth that predominates in youth, and approximates more to a friendship model of loving.

PASSIONATE LOVE

- **The experiences are intense**
- **There is little middle ground**
- **There is great joy or tremendous pain**

vs. COMPANIONATE LOVE

- **The partners are friends**
- **Every day life is a part of the relationship**
- **There is stability**

As I have pointed out before—as is often pointed out, in fact—the divorce rate in the U. S. is over half. When marriages fail, it is acutely painful for many women. The hope of finding someone else, of getting it right this time, prevails, but the repercussion of having made a mistake and having lost those precious years of one's life is haunting and recurrent. Author Shere Hite finds in her book *Women and Love: A Cultural Revolution in Progress* that 59 percent of her interviewees stated that "passionate love cannot last" and 54 percent preferred the stability of loving, caring feelings over being passionately in love. No matter how wonderful it can feel to be in love, 69 percent of married women and 47 percent of single women say they have decided they do not like, or no longer trust, being in love—it is too volatile, too dangerous. And if they had to choose between passion and stability, 58 percent of Hite's pool will take a relationship that works on a day-to-day basis.

"After two divorces, I am definitely looking for someone who is secure with himself, who makes me feel safe," Terri, who is 41, begins her interview. "I do not want another screwed-up marriage but a solid, strong friendship. I see now that in both of my past marriages, they began well, but fell apart rather quickly. Both relationships were so destructive because there was never any foundation. There were wild times and very romantic interludes, then a crash and burn. After a while, I couldn't get enough sustenance from the good parts to see me through each work week.

"My biggest mistake was that I wanted to be anchored and I thought that marriage would do the trick. That is why I married twice. I was a party girl and I wanted a home life. I was afraid of myself without a semblance of normalcy so I had to be married. But there was nothing safe about my marriages because there was no true sharing. What I know now is that in order to have a home life, the marriage has to be about the mundane, about the give-and-take of regular life. I really think I read too many magazines and I mistakenly thought that you had to be madly in love with your husband. That works at the very start, but no one warned me about later on. Those kinds of feelings wear thin very quickly when there are bills and a mortgage to pay. I have no illusions today because of my second divorce. After pretending twice, I had to come to my senses. I had to take stock of what happened and why it happened. Deep down I know I'll always believe in the perfect romantic relationship but I won't be fooled again."

Until a woman is informed, either through group therapy, individual therapy, or even by having heart-to-heart discussions with close female friends, she is likely to repeat her pattern with a new partner. It is only if there is a crisis, or she has simply been at it too long, as in the case of Terri, that a woman successfully avoids making the same mistake again. At this stage, she begins to pay more attention to herself, and her values may change as a result.

"It is complicated for women," according to psychotherapist Brenda Szulman, "who marry early, and have not learned about themselves. They are more susceptible to repeating their histories and to the myth of marrying an ideal soulmate." These women are still inebriated by this myth, which stems from fairy tales and from the media.

SEX WANES

While the intimacy and closeness may grow, sexual intimacy in many marriages decreases with time. Eventually this takes a toll on the marriage.

"Sex is a big part of this marriage," Andrea tells us, "because it is a new marriage and because we are in our early forties and want to hold onto that feeling. I also see it as an expression of our love, which sounds corny but it is true. It reminds me of when I was with my college boyfriend, except of course we are adults and so there is a maturity to the relationship. I have friends who feign headaches with their husbands and are not interested in sex anymore. They will tell me that it is overrated, or that they are too tired to be bothered. I can't imagine this ever happening here, and I know, having been single for a time, that I'm so lucky that the rest of the marriage falls into place. Or maybe the sex falls into place because the rest of the marriage works."

In reality, sex does take a back seat to the demands of life. Just as women hold onto the notion of romantic love, the idea of sex in love and marriage is very significant for them. So while women may stop feeling sexy, or be too exhausted once there are children, the idea of romantic love, including sexual intimacy, still matters. Here, then, is another example of how women are not prepared for the real world; they do not expect that sex will become one more requirement on the list of wifely responsibilities. They yearn for it and the idealized love it represents, and simultaneously lose interest in the actual act because they are on overload.

"I know that working two shifts and aiming to please my husband was not easy," Marlene, 47, admits. At the age of 33, she saw her sex life languish. "I let it go. Something had to give because I was so tired and he didn't look so sexy in his torn, dirty bathrobe when I got home from work. I felt I wasn't taken care of, so why should there be sex? It just exhausted me further. And without it, we just moved away from each other. Sex is definitely a connection. In the end my husband had an affair and I look back on it and realize I wasn't available for him, and I wasn't available for me.

"This affair he had woke me up. I knew I wanted my husband and I wanted our marriage to work. He was traveling and away several nights a week. This had to stop. I knew I had to be happier with myself in order to be happier in the marriage. I took the cue from the affair, as hard as that was, and I worked on getting us back together. I remembered us as newlyweds, before all the responsibilities took over. I told my husband the truth, that I couldn't slip on a teddy after one of our children had puked on me. It wasn't possible, but it wasn't the only thing we wanted or needed. Slowly my husband and I put it back together and began to take care of each other again. For me this is a triumph because it was so painful, so awkward–and forgiving was not easy."

Marriage is defined as an exclusive commitment to a partner, which entails fidelity. But as women become wives and mothers, many times their sexuality is lost or buried. What made the relationship exciting sexually is almost forgotten, and when sexual energy is no longer put into the marriage, the marriage suffers. Men have been viewed as more preoccupied with sex than women, and consequently, there are those men who will find satisfying sex elsewhere, even though they value their marriage. A marriage is comprised of sexual and psychic intimacy. Psychic intimacy is the part of a marriage where both partners share their innermost thoughts. Sexual intimacy is of another order, and does not demand psychic intimacy; it does not even require a commitment.

NAVIGATING INTIMACY

Later in life women are better equipped to recognize their needs in a marriage. The depth of intimacy and commitment is up to them.

The lustful stage of a relationship fades rather quickly and then we are left with the more profound aspects of marriage, those of intimacy and commitment. Assuming we are committed to the marriage, are we able to hold on to the energy which intimacy and love relationships require in the context of hectic, overloaded lifestyles? The fact is that women in their midlife are in a position to negotiate, and today's society, however tied to the past, is becoming more understanding of any new arrangement a couple comes to. The hope is that a woman will be more self-aware and therefore better empowered to define the terms of her relationship.

4

In the Driver's Seat: The Affair

"I was in an unhappy marriage for thirteen years before I had an affair," explains Natalie. "I did it because I knew of no other escape. I have two sons and there is no way I would be divorced. My lover is so unlike my husband and that is the best part for me. We spent hours together and we are confidants. My husband would never listen to me and this man listens. My husband and I are the same age and Luke, my lover, is ten years older than I am. He is a professor and my husband is a contractor. I enjoy conversations with Luke, whereas my husband is very quiet and mostly he watches sports events on television when he comes home. This affair is about opposite men in opposite worlds. It has been going on for two years now and I am much happier since it started.

"If anyone had ever predicted that I would have a lover and stay in my marriage, I would have thought they were nuts. I have always seen myself as moral and honest. I had been faithful in this marriage even during my most unhappy days, until I met my Luke. In a sense I feel I deserve this relationship because it makes me lighthearted and my marriage is such a downer, so loaded with bad things. I see my affair as a great escape and also as a way of facing what I can't have in the marriage and have to found with another man. I am totally attached to my lover but I will not leave the marriage."

There is little question that married women who take lovers are both crying out for help and reclaiming themselves as they do it. When I first began eight years ago to research the phenomenon of women who engage in extramarital affairs for my book, *A Passion for More: Wives Reveal the Affairs That Make or Break Their Marriages,* there were many people resistant to the idea. For centuries men have been allowed to conduct extracurriculars, but women have been expected to be chaste and loyal. The notion that women also could be party to duplicity and infidelity for the very same reasons or for reasons unique to them was largely ignored.

Statistics on married women who take lovers vary greatly. The survey on extramarital affairs published in the February 2001 edition of *Esquire* indicates that more married women have engaged in affairs than unwed men. While their percentages seem relatively low—28 percent of women and 26 percent of men—the fact that women surpass men in this regard is intriguing. My own research consisted of interviews with hundreds of women across the country, of various ages and from different walks of life. The results were startling and enlightening and showed that over 60 percent of married women engage in extramarital affairs. I have found that these affairs can be classified into four groups: self-esteem affairs, sex-driven affairs, love affairs, and empowering affairs.

TYPES OF AFFAIRS

- **Self-Esteem Affairs. These affairs make women feel better about themselves as they age and lose confidence in their marriages**

- **Sex-Driven Affairs. Women take lovers for the same reason that men do—for sex and pleasure**

- **Love Affairs. Unexpectedly a woman falls in love with another man. When a marriage has true intimacy, this rarely happens**

- **Empowering Affairs. These trysts empower women—they approach them with a sense of entitlement**

When the Kinsey Report came out in 1953, the news that 26 percent of women reported having sex outside of the marriage shocked the nation. Thirty-four years later, Shere Hite's book *Women in Love: A Cultural Revolution* reported that 70 percent of married women participated in a relationships outside a marriage. Whatever the discrepancy in statistics, the phenomenon persists. A woman who begins an affair is reclaiming herself through the relationship with her lover. It is not only about the lover, but how she feels when she is with him.

The prejudice against married women who pursue extramarital affairs is still widespread in the United States. According to a 1996 study by Adler, 70 percent of Americans view sex outside a marriage as detrimental to the marriage. Masters, Johnson and Kolodny, sexologists, report that extramarital sex has not diminished even with the threat of AIDS. In my research, which is not a statistical study but based on personal stories, the major motivation to stray comes from loneliness in the marriage. And while studies indicate that the double standard holds true, women today, more than ever before, are willing and ready to take lovers who satisfy their needs. The conventional wisdom about the gender differences in having affairs is that men do it because they are programmed to spread their seed. Women, on the other hand, are not interested in casual flings but in having babies and a partner to father their children. This supposition, however, does not hold true, and the expectation for women to marry and have children is being challenged by many women. In the same manner as men, women who are married and unhappy may seek a lover to meet their needs.

LOVERS FILL THE EMPTINESS

- **Women partake in extramarital affairs when the marriage is lacking**

- **There is a double standard for men and women who have affairs**

- **Our culture creates an easy environment for extramarital affairs for men and women both.**

Extramarital affairs have long been a popular theme in literature and film, news and magazine articles. We are well aware of the fact that both Prince Charles and the late Princess Diana engaged in affairs during their marriage. Charles' long standing affair with Camilla Parker Bowles was the cause of Diana and Charles' subsequent divorce. Robert James Waller's bestselling novel, and popular film starring Meryl Streep and Clint Eastwood, *The Bridges of Madison County*, evokes our sympathy for a woman who is married and falls madly in love with a stranger. Her decision to stay in a less-than-optimal marriage for the sake of her children is something she is seen to regret for the rest of her life. For Francesca Johnson, the heroine of the novel, the connection to her lover, Robert Kincaid, only highlights what is missing in her marriage. This is often the case: the affair is a wake-up call to the woman, who is forced to assess her situation. She may leave with the lover or leave on her own. Or she may use the affair to improve her marriage, with a better understanding of what she can or cannot have with her husband.

"I have had several affairs in my marriage," admits Donna, who at 50 is married with two children. "I never contemplated leaving for any of these men, but they made feel special and life became more exciting during the affair. It was a reaction to my husband, who is very involved in his business and travels frequently. I did it for me, it was something outside my life with kids and soccer games, car pools and catechism. I cannot say if I would do it again or not, but I have no regrets about having done it so far.

"In the end, you are only cheating yourself though, because an affair takes its toll on the marriage. When we marry, we do not really comprehend that we will live and sleep with this man for the rest of our lives. And, these days, we live a long time! Women live even longer than men, by an average of seven years. Having children only complicates the marriage as far as romance goes, in my opinion. There is no way to have a romance and to raise children at the same time. These lovers were not about friendship or companionship for me, they were about feeling beautiful and young. I need to be convinced that somehow life was not passing me by because these men wanted me. I know that some women fall in love with another man during the marriage, but I never had that problem. I always saw an affair as a way to get through. In the end, it only makes one realize how confining life is, and how single-minded we've been taught to be."

When women have affairs to feel better about themselves and to stave off the inevitable march of time and the aging process, they do not seem to be emotionally invested in the relationship. It is much easier for these women to detach and move on to the next lover, if they so choose, or to simply stop and revise the marriage without the embellishment of the lover. While Donna seems to be detached enough to protect herself, there are those women who can be destroyed emotionally by an affair, and whose world can be turned upside down.

AFFAIRS FOR SELF-ESTEEM

- **Women want to feel beautiful and**

appreciated

- **The lover is not about commitment but excitement**

- **Serial lovers are a possibility**

In Sheila's case, having an affair represented an intimate bond with her lover which caused her tremendous pain in her marriage. Rather than being empowered by her affair, she began to lose her center. "I did not expect to become involved with anyone during my marriage," begins Sheila, who at 37 has three small children. "Last year I met a man at work who absolutely swept me off my feet. I don't think that I was ever really in love with my husband, but I hadn't considered it that important. We have three children under the age of six, and a brand-new house. There is no way that a person can become introspective leading this kind of life. Mostly I am trying to get through each day. I work part time and the kids are all in some kind of school program. But when I met this man, everything changed. I became obsessed with him. And at first, I became more aware of myself and my needs. I saw how awful my marriage is, and I admitted to myself how trapped I am.

"My lover is very young and very fit. He is a single guy without any responsibilities. His work matters to him, but he is not consumed by it like my husband, and he doesn't hide behind it. We laugh together and share a kind of bond. I feel that I am very attached to him. Also I see no future and it makes me sad. I spend hours missing him and waiting for his phone calls. The futility of it all is ruining me. We are from such different worlds, I can't imagine anything good coming of this. It only makes me want to run away, and with three small children where would I go?"

Women who fall in love with their lovers may be falling in love with the idea of the independence and romance that he represents. Even if their lives are fraught with the demands of husbands, children, work, and homes to run, the lover is worth the effort. A woman who is overwhelmed—especially a woman in her thirties or forties who has not had any fun in a long while—will find this secret rendezvous fulfilling. Those women/wives who operate on automatic pilot—who sleepwalk—as a means to handle their responsibilities might find themselves rejuvenated through this connection to a lover.

LOVERS AS AN ESCAPE

- **Women become attached when their lives feel devoid of hope**
- **Women become attached when their lives are on overload**
- **Women become attached when they are operating on automatic pilot**

"Lovers and husbands are like apples and oranges," Dr. Ronnie Burak points out. "When a woman is with her lover, there are no concerns for mortgage payments and tuition bills. It is a fantasy world based on romance. If a woman marries her lover, it often becomes more of the same and now the lover simply steps into the shoes of the husband, and everyday life resumes." Out of my pool of interviewees, 25 percent have left

their husbands and married their lovers, 45 percent have remained with their husbands. Fifty-five percent have left the
marriage, and of this number, 25 percent have left for the lover,
while 30 percent have left for themselves. Whatever path a
woman chooses once she has encountered this other partner,
her life is irreversibly changed and her sense of self is altered
and often enhanced.

Romantic love is idealized in our society, and women thrive
on it. We expect it to last through years of marriage and the
drudgery of the day-to-day routine. At the same time, women
are fortifying themselves, staking out their turf in every way
possible—be it in the workplace, in a relationship, with friends
and family, or in a marriage. An affair can actually strengthen a
marriage in the long run. There are many more avenues open
to married women today and the choice to have a lover is
merely one of them. Yet in choosing this route, we have to face
up to some repercussions.

Often an affair may be a way to complement the marriage,
so that the lover plus husband could ideally add up to one
man who is satisfying. What seems most remarkable to me as
a chronicler of women's lives is how much less women seem to
worry about the aftermath of an affair than they did in the
past—even as recently as eight or ten years ago. Women are
greater risk takers than ever before, and this applies to the
threat of divorce as well. All states in America permit no-fault
divorces, and most are no-fault exclusively. Even in fault divorces, adultery is not always verified. An affair, if one is exposed, may become a wake-up call for the husband, who often
wants to save the marriage. Shere Hite 's survey indicates that

60 percent of men who discover their wives having an affair are willing to work on the marriage. This belies the picture of the stereotypical husband who has historically divorced his wife because of her infidelity.

Brondi Borer, a divorce attorney in New York City, tells us that adultery is rarely used in and of itself as grounds for divorce. "Although New York state is a fault state, adultery is difficult to prove and witnesses are required," says Borer. "An interesting aspect of adultery and divorce is that if a man knows that his wife is having an affair, and does nothing about it for years, he cannot use it against her in the divorce. His knowledge of the affair is tantamount to condoning it. So statistically speaking, there are very few divorce cases in New York State that invoke adultery as grounds. When the real story comes out, more times than not both partners had someone on the side during the marriage."

"I never worried about getting caught because I was careful," Emilie tells us, having conducted an affair while her husband was overseas for eighteen months. "I thought about myself, not him. I was not getting my needs met and then I met a man. Maybe I should not have been married so early–eight years ago, when I was in my mid-twenties. Maybe I should have walked the other way when I met this man. But I didn't, I got to know him. And for a year, I was with this man every day. My rationale was that if my husband learned about it, it would teach him a thing or two. After all, women are always learning about their husbands' affairs and then running to the diet doctor, the gym, or to get breast implants. This time it was the opposite and I was in charge."

Collette, at 35, found herself on the more familiar side of an extramarital affair for a woman when she discovered that her husband was conducting one. She decided to work to salvage her marriage.

"I was married for ten years with four kids when I learned that my husband, Doug, was having an affair," Collette explains. "I was devastated. Whatever had gone on in the marriage, I never expected this. I knew it happened because my husband traveled for work and also because four small children are very demanding. Still, it didn't make me feel any better. I confronted him and he confessed. I even saw them together at a club.

"I had to assess what mattered to me most, and that was the marriage. While I felt he was tainted after the affair and that it had infected our marriage, I also knew we had to move ahead. That meant I had to take a long look at myself and what I was doing wrong. I had lost my sense of humor and I was exhausted. I had two jobs to hold down and all these children and an absent husband. I couldn't be romantic and sexy like the other woman, that was beyond me. But I could try in other ways—I could be more available to my husband and less worried about the kids all the time. I decided to hire a sitter once a week so that we could get out alone. My husband's affair actually gave me incentive to try harder."

Our culture has taught us that men cheat for lust or for a sexual thrill, while women more often cheat for emotional satisfaction. This has always been the standard and the accepted reason. Antoinette Michaels, relationship expert, points out that women are looking for romance in a relationship outside the marriage. "Women give sex in an affair in exchange for the fantasy of a knight in shining armor. Most men are not involved emotionally and there is little fantasy about being swept off their feet. For them, it is about getting away with something and about the sheer high of cheating." Yet in recent years, there is an evolution in the reasons why women choose their lovers. Women who are between the ages of 30 and 40 often admit to the same inducement that has conventionally applied to men. These wives are in search of a sexual encounter. Perhaps their generation has fewer expectations than babyboomer wives, and is more open to experience. For certain they are less concerned with the consequences–to the marriage and to their own mental state.

BABYBOOMERS

Babyboomers have suffered for their idealized image of love and marriage. The women/wives are disappointed and disenchanted. Their vulnerability and neediness may manifest in an extramarital affair.

vs. 30- to 40-YEAR-OLD WOMEN

These women who were born after the babyboomers have a more realistic expectation of love and marriage. If they are not completely happy, an extramarital affair is not necessarily an emotional investment but another option available.

The recent film *The Contender* starring Joan Allen as Laine Hanson, a Senator who is chosen by the President (Jeff Bridges) to be his Vice President, addresses the issue of infidelity. While Laine Hanson is under scrutiny, it is revealed that she had an affair with a married man who was her campaign manager and who later became her husband. This brings us to another aspect of affair, the role of injured spouse. Actress Mariel Hemingway portrays the first wife as bereft and betrayed. The question, in these triangles, is whether there is any solidarity among women.

When married women are unfaithful, they become "the other woman." This certainly puts a spin on the cliché of the other woman as a single secretary named Gloria, who works long hours at the office and is an insidious seductress. In my book, *The Men Out There: A Woman's Little Black Book*, there is a chapter on the married man as potential partner. Both points of view—that of the wife and that of the other woman—are explored. The wife tries to keep the marriage together but the infidelity is an invisible weight for her. Deep within, she knows the marriage is lacking but she hangs on because it is the only security she knows. The other woman offers her lover—someone else's husband, in these instances—a secret universe. And because she feels chosen, she waits, to see what will happen. The fact is, this "other woman" might not be married, with her own husband hanging on to a failed marriage, and wishing the affair would end and the status quo be reinstated. Thus, affairs are not always gender-specific, but triangulated by definition. And these triangles each has its own history.

"Who knows if a man would react so strongly to the breakup of his marriage," comments Brenda Szulman, psychotherapist. "Men tend to put one foot in front of the other while women can be devastated by a breakup or the discovery of an affair. But what happens more frequently now is that instead of concentrating on the breakup, whatever the circumstances, women are not shutting down but looking to start life again and to rebound. If anything, a rejected woman should grieve and mourn, then re-emerge."

"After I learned that my husband was having an affair over the internet, I filed for divorce," said Tammy, who is 33, "I didn't really blame this woman, I blamed all of us, my husband, her and me. I just wanted to move on and not worry about what had been. I wouldn't do it to someone else's husband, but maybe she didn't even know that he was married. If she thinks that she is more powerful than I am, I don't see it that way. And I don't think she won. I just think that we all make mistakes.

"My hope is that I will get over this and meet someone new. My eyes are wide-open now. I don't know if I can trust anyone. On the other hand, at least women are getting what they want, even if it's sometimes at the expense of another woman."

In her essay entitled "Sexuality," Catharine A. Mackinnon writes that sexuality is a "social construct of male power: defined by men, forced on women, and constitutive of the meaning of gender... Feminist theory becomes a project of analyzing that situation in order to face it for what it is, in order to change it." It is a fine line which married women walk by not taking a lover for their own pleasure while they are in a marriage. It is equally tricky for a single woman who becomes involved with a man who is already married. In each of these scenarios, women are behaving more boldly than in the past, and with an impressive sense of entitlement. A strong moral code may or may not determine whether to proceed.

ENTITLEMENT EMERGES

Women are beginning to see themselves as entitled to more in all areas of their lives. An affair is one form of expression. One's moral standard still may cast over a shadow over the relationship.

"I did not mind that I was having an affair at first," admits Bethany. "I justified it as a way to take care of my needs. And I was contemplating leaving my husband anyway. But after a few months, I no longer wanted to see pictures of Ed's kids, nor of his house. Every time we got together I felt sorry for his wife. The odd part is, I rarely thought about my own marriage. I knew it wasn't working and that the affair was simply a byproduct of that. One time I was looking at his boys' faces in a photograph and I knew I didn't want to be responsible for the breakup of that family. I believe that Ed loved us both, his wife and me. I wrestled with this for another year. We spoke about it and he suggested that I issue an ultimatum. That wasn't my style. Either he wanted to leave for himself or it was no good. I was not going to break up a family because I was in love with a man.

"In the end I left my husband and took my kids with me. My ex-husband found someone very quickly while I tried for years to get over my lover. What he did was help me see what I could have. The sad part is he couldn't be the one who was there for me in the final analysis."

Harold Pinter's play *Betrayal* depicts a love triangle between Emma, her lover Jerry, and her husband Robert. Jerry and Robert are old, best friends. Still the affair between Jerry and Emma lasts for seven years, and while it runs its course, children are born and raised, and the fathers' paternity is never challenged. Betrayals surround the characters, since Jerry suspects his wife, Judith, whom we never see, of having an affair, and Robert confesses to Emma that he has been adulterous throughout the marriage. There is a remarkable lack of guilt on Emma's part when she confesses to Robert that she is involved romantically with Jerry. Since both Jerry and Robert, as lover and husband, seem to suit Emma's disparate needs, one can imagine that a blend of the two men into one would be her consummate man. It is as if both the lover and husband enable her—she gets from one what she cannot get from the other.

As indicated earlier, there are no dependable statistics on the percentage of married women who engage in extramarital affairs, and the situation for men is no better. Yet having listened to the stories that women confided in me, I believe that the percentage of married women who take on another relationship is close to 60 percent. This 'mini-survey' falls somewhere between a January 1999 poll conducted by women.com, which reported that 41 percent of women under 30 had engaged in an affair, and Shere Hite's survey in *Women in Love: A*

Cultural Revolution in Progress, which reports that 70 percent of women married for over five years have sex outside their marriage. Pam Gerhardt, in a *Washington Post* article, "The Emotional Cost of Infidelity," on March 30, 1999, gave a very tentative figure of 25 to 70 percent for all males and 15 to 60 percent for women, although she also comments that the "statistics on the frequency of affairs don't add up."

Shere Hite's stunning research indicates that women believe in fidelity even as they take on lovers, which they do for pleasure, and because they feel alienated and lonely in the marriages. These are not only women immersed in their careers who meet men in the workplace or those engaged in an open marriage (of which there are very few), but all kinds of women, from cities, towns, and countryside alike. None of these women seems concerned with AIDS, because the women believe they know their partners and these unions are not random, but planned. Another reason women take lovers is that sex diminishes in the marriage, which can happen for a myriad of reasons.

There is little question that women feel much less guilty than formerly once they find the "other man," who is most often the opposite of the husband and offers the woman a completely dissimilar experience. Those women who are "in love" with their husbands as opposed to "loving" them are least likely to have an affair, with a solid 98-percent fidelity rate, according to Hite. And so it seems that women who are "in love" with their husbands are in touch with their own needs and are satisfied with the choice they have made.

INFIDELITY FOR WOMEN

- **Somewhere between 41% and 70% of married women have had sex outside the marriage**
- **Women have affairs because of the loneliness in the marriage**
- **Younger women look for sexual experiences**
- **Women of all ages who are "in love" with their husbands are faithful**

Infidelity among men is another matter, and, again, while there are no completely reliable studies, Hite findings show us a 72-percent population of husbands having extramarital sex. Ironically, 79 percent of the women in Hite's study did not suspect their husbands or lovers of being unfaithful, and for those women who are involved in their own relationships with the "other man" there co-exists a dogged belief in their husbands' fidelity. Denial is a form of "sleepwalking," where women will not face what is unpleasant or unacceptable if they have no power to change it.

INFIDELITY FOR MEN

- **Hite reports that 72% of husbands have extramarital sex**
- **79% of the women in her pool do not believe their husbands are unfaithful**
- **70% of the women do believe that**

their lovers are faithful

- **For centuries men have been ex-
  cused for their indiscretions**

"I knew that my husband, George, cheated because he cheated on me when we were dating. And he had cheated on his girlfriend before me. But I put it out of my head because I really wanted to be his wife," Jessie, at 33, begins her interview. "One night I called him on his cell phone and a woman answered. I think she was as surprised to hear my voice as I was to hear hers. I don't know why George would do that, let her use the phone when it's how I reach him when he travels. Anyway, that was when I knew. I asked him about it when he came home and for three years afterwards, I asked.

"One night he came home late, as usual, and he asked me why I stopped accusing him of cheating. I said I didn't know. But I suppose I did–I stopped caring and I was already thinking that I was young still and that there was a world out there. I didn't necessarily want to divorce or have an affair, but I was starting to think differently. I was beginning to worry about me and not about him. That is where I'm at now. My suspicions of George's cheating chipped away at the marriage. There was no way I could justify it, even if he was on a business trip. It wasn't what I wanted and I hated that nagging feeling that he was doing something wrong where the marriage was concerned."

Infidelity is such a fascinating, unending subject that women's magazines cover it on a monthly basis, and the internet offers websites for every member of the triangle: the other woman, the injured spouse and the unfaithful spouse. From each point of view, the motivation is understandable and complicated. In recent years the fascination of affairs has been extended to internet affairs. While ten or fifteen years ago an affair of the mind consisted of a interlude with a colleague at work or someone one might meet on a train or plane, the internet extends one's options, and cyberspace affairs are on the rise. In *Redbook* magazine, May 2000, this sensation is described in an article by Lesley Dormen entitled "Chat-room Cheating?" Virtual infidelity, as it may be described, has all the elements of real-life infidelity and the partners are every bit as consumed with the relationship. As the rate of spouses who have met on the internet grows, we have to assume that the rate of extramarital affairs via internet increases as well. "Is e-mail between two amorous people truly, as some correspondents seem to imagine, a modern version of old-fashioned courtship letters?" asks Dormen, who quotes psychotherapist Jane Greer. Greer views internet intimacy as "false and anonymous, like sharing your life story with someone you meet on a chairlift." Nonetheless, there are married women who have become involved with men via the internet and find their lives completely turned around in the process.

"I have never met my lover in person," sighs Sheri, "but we e-mail each other many times a day. When I don't hear from him I feel deflated and when I get a great e-mail, I'm thrilled. I don't know how long I'll last without spending time with him, but maybe that will be a disappointment after what we share over the internet. We do not talk on the phone but communicate only by e-mail. Some of these letters are quite romantic and some are sexy. People at work have noticed that since this cyberspace affair began, I am always on the computer. If I go out for a meeting, I will race back to check my e-mail. Both of us are married, but it seems besides the point in our case.

"I'm not sure that I would do something like this if it didn't exist in space because it feels different, I feel like I am doing nothing wrong. Even the written word does not seem incriminating in the form of e-mail. Perhaps I am naive, but I feel like one day this affair will grow into the greatest relationship of my life."

Jane also has faith in her cyberspace romance, and the fact that she has only met her lover twice does not deter her. Having been married for eight years, she is now ready to leave her husband for her internet lover. Although Jane is "reclaiming" herself through this process, the result with the internet lover remains unpredictable.

"I don't get to see Mitch at all, but it almost doesn't matter because the relationship works over the internet. I am 38 years old and I have been married twice but this is the first time I have really felt good about the person I am with. Something always comes up when we make plans to get together and at first I was very disappointed, but as the relationship goes on, it seems less important.

"Having an affair without physical contact is all about passion, emotion, and idealization. We are not together physically but our lives are entwined. He and I met through a business transaction and his child knows about me and my kids know about him as business associates. I will sometimes pick up something for his daughter and he will for my boys and mail it to them. In this way, it seems that we've gone beyond cyperspace, and have entered each other's lives. His wife knows about me as a business contact as well, and my husband knows vaguely about it. He isn't really interested in my life, which is probably why I'm having this affair. Being with Mitch, via cyperspace, has definitely influenced me about my marriage. I now feel ready to go. My hope is that this relationship will become physical in time, and that we will become a part of each other's lives in every way. For now, we e-mail each other three or four times a day.

"If I don't get a reply, I feel disappointed and hurt. He seems to do better with this because he is not as passionate or as romantic about us. When he gets that way, I love it. I am facing that the future is unknown and having seen Mitch only two times is unquestionably strange. But this takes more work, in a different way. He loves my messages and I have to be quite clever and creative. It isn't like being in the same room with someone or in the same bed. Our reactions to each other are mental and not physical and it requires energy to convey your feelings without touching and without sex."

Lacking physical intimacy, the validity of the connection has to be questioned. There is no doubt that cyperspace love is another version of an affair of the mind, but the immediacy of e-mail and its accessibility can cause it to become a central part of one's life. Yet because these two people have never interacted, except by e-mail, there are large pieces of the relationship that are missing. A liaison such as this can fall into the infatuation category. As Robert J. Sternberg defines it in his essay "Triangulating Love," infatuation is "love that turns toward obsession with the partner being loved as an idealized object rather than as him or herself." In fact, when a person is infatuated with someone, there is no intimacy and no commitment. Since the partner becomes idealized, and cannot be seen for who s/he really is. Infatuations can be obsessive, according to Sternberg. "One can be devoured or consumed by the love, so that it ends up taking time, energy, and motivation from other things in one's life." If a woman wakes up only to find herself in an untenable, disappointing situation again, she has not achieved her goal. Only if she can be discerning in cyberspace or otherwise will she profit from the results.

AFFAIRS IN CYBERSPACE

- **The two partners may never meet**
- **Intimacy is a missing ingredient in the relationship**
- **Infatuation plays a key part in the attachment**
- **If they do meet, their illusions are often shattered**

Whether we condemn or condone extramarital affairs, they exist, and will continue to exist. It seems a social fiction that women, like men, remain in a marriage for many years without having a wandering eye. On some level, it has been dependency that has kept women in a marriage without straying, for fear of being caught and let loose in a cruel world. Divorce laws work more in a woman's favor today than ever before, according to Brondi Borer, divorce attorney, and with the financial freedom which careers offer women, there seems to be less at stake and more to gain from the experience of having a lover.

When an affair leads to divorce, there can be anger and resentment on the part of the rejected partner. Not every husband becomes introspective when he learns of his wife's infidelity. If the affair is the result of a workplace tryst, a husband may feel doubly cheated–his wife has met someone else and she is now in an arena that was historically preserved for men. Over and over, I was struck by the fact that what really upset a man who discovered his wife straying was not the emotional attachment she had made with another, but their sexual acting out. This was usually the occasion for out-of-control, violent scenes, and drastic, on-the-spot decisions that their marriage together was effectively over. Marital sex seemed to exist within a circle of fire so far as the husband was concerned, and if his wife breached that boundary with another the marriage was finished–and he was ready to abandon her to the wolves.

Men, for their part, have been permitted to fall in love with someone else, whether the affair stems from travel or the office. Women, for the past thirty years, were left at home to care for children and housekeeping, without autonomy. Today, those working wives are exposed to and tantalized by the very same opportunities their male counterparts have. The U. S. Census reports that in 1997 there were 63 million women in the workplace, with 61 percent of this population married. Married status aside, the chance to become romantically involved with a co-worker increases significantly as the numbers increase. If women are not in the workplace, or if they work part time, there are other choices available in terms of an extracurricular. If someone is motivated to meet her lover, there is always day care for young children.

WORKPLACE AFFAIRS

- **61% of working women are married**
- **Women are now similarly positioned in the world as men**
- **Business trips, expense accounts, freedom are all the currency traditionally traded by men**

vs.

EXTRACURRICULARS

- **Children attend day care**
- **Older children are in school all day**
- **Women are in search of self-expression**

"I know that my job gave me the confidence to have an affair," explains Elysee who at 40 has been working for the past five years. "I felt so isolated and bored in the suburbs, and

I wanted to finish my degree and get a job. As soon as my youngest was in kindergarten, I did just that. I met my lover at work and because it felt like an equal playing field, I was open to it. I suspect that all those years spent baking cookies and making bologna sandwiches made me feel starved for experiences. And while I never would have dreamed of it before I got a career, once I did get there, I asked myself why not.

"I feel like my life is complete now. I have my two kids and my husband. I drive to work every day and I'm in an environment I enjoy and I am respected for my work. I see my lover every few days and it is perfect. He is a single guy but I know one day he'll want to have what I have, a family, a house, children. For now it is so easy and I try not to think of the future. I know that we enrich each other's lives, and that we have only brought out the best in each other. I view the world in a new way since I met him—I feel like I'm young and anything is possible." There are those women who use a splitting mechanism that enables them to be both lover and wife. On those days when they are with their husbands and/or children, they are the good wife/good mother. On those days when they see their lover, these women are engrossed in the romantic life with him. This dual approach may last for months or years, depending on the duration of the affair. Some women move from one lover to another, following the same pattern many men have done, and there are those who experience one isolated episode. What matters most is how it affects the women, and what impact it has on their lives.

SPLITTING MECHANISMS

- **Women find they can be both wife and a lover**
- **The dual roles could last for years**
- **Women compartmentalize to maintain this lifestyle**

My research indicates that 65 percent of all women experienced better sex with their lover than their husband. Seventy percent of the women said their lover and their husbands are opposites, with each man contributing uniquely to the woman's life. Yet the lover is more often the catalyst, rather than the cause, to leave. The lover is viewed as an escape in 40 percent of the cases, and 60 percent perceive the lover as a wake-up call. Only 25 percent of the women marry their lover. Amazingly enough, 90 percent of the women have no guilt; instead they feel entitled to the affair and what pleasure it brings into their lives.

MINI-SURVEY RESULTS

- **65% report the sex is better with the lover**
- **70% say the lover is the opposite of the husband**
- **25% marry their lover**
- **40% realize the lover is an escape**
- **60% view the lover as a wake-up call**

• 90% of the women are guiltless, and feel entitled to the affair

And so the myth of the vulnerable woman, trained to be deeply committed to marriage and home, is dispelled. Men as rescuers, false and true, are everywhere, and it is curious where a woman takes her life after the affair. She may divorce and marry again, or if she leaves a troubled marriage and the affair was a symptom but not a cure, she has taken the first step to self-confrontation. The real question is, will she repeat her pattern, or will she take her newfound wisdom and apply it to the next chapter in her life? In *The Creation of the Feminist Consciousness*, historian Gerda Lerner writes that the monopoly which men have had over women has decreased to a degree. "Women do not as yet have power over institutions, over the state, over the law," writes Lerner. "But the theoretical insights modern feminist scholarship has already achieved have the power to shatter the patriarchal paradigm." We are reminded that with this progress come more choices for women, in every aspect of their lives. The extramarital affair is merely one form of expression. The choices women make in the aftermath of an affair are what put them on another course.

After writing *A Passion for More*, I was asked repeatedly why women have affairs instead of putting that energy into their marriages. It is when women no longer feel motivated to look to the marriage for pleasure, excitement or contentment that they consider an affair and it becomes an alternative. Everyday life absolutely tests the romantic elements of a marriage. The initial excitement fades and is replaced with drudgery and ongoing obligations. If a comfort level is not achieved in marriage once the romance and sexiness has faded, this causes a rift. The choice is to retrieve what has waned in the marriage, or seek it elsewhere. For those women who sense a hopelessness in their connection to their husbands, and do not believe that closeness can exist, the lover fills the void. If nothing else, the lover is a wake-up mechanism for these women; the affair represents freedom and power for women to utilize however they see fit.

5

Uncharted Waters: Divorce and Singlehood

"Being divorced made me feel like a marked woman," begins Brett. "I never really knew how the world perceived divorced women until I became one. I had friends who told me to stay away from their husbands, as if I wanted any of them. Other friends wanted to know the scoop when my divorce was first announced and wanted to meet some of my more serious dates, but they didn't care about what I was going through, what I was experiencing. Eventually I realized I had to get through this on my own, because becoming divorced is a strenuous, painful process. On the other end, I was not the same. I felt like I was getting myself back, but to the rest of the world, I was not the same. My quality of life had been diminished, I had my children part time and I took a job. That was the first phase.

"Later I began to date, something I had never done before since I was married so young. It was shocking to be a single person after all these years invested in married life. It took me a while to be courageous and to be fixed up. It seemed to me that my single friends were dying to be married, or remarried. I cared less and I took my time. I met a lot of people. I forced myself to listen to them, almost like it was an interview. I'd never been so careful before, but I didn't want to make the same mistake again."

For many of us who believed that marriage was a cure-all for every ill and that their pursuits and dreams came after those of our husband's and children's, there is the task of rediscovering ourselves and re-ordering priorities. Divorce is an arduous and daunting task that forever changes us and our status. Even if we go on to marry again, the divorce has scarred us. We approach life in another way; our self-perception and view of the world are altered. We see our children in another light, because in the process they have become children of divorce.

Coupling (and recoupling) is an age-old theme in our society, one in which marriage and family are seen as central to our lives. This, however, is evolving, as the late Daniel J. Levinson noted in his book, *The Seasons of a Woman's Life*. "We live in a time when the Traditional Marriage Enterprise, and the gender meanings, values and social structures that support it, are undergoing major change," he writes. "The homemakers' lives give evidence that the traditional pattern is difficult to sustain." When the traditional homemaker compares herself to the career woman, she feels that she has forfeited opportunities by staying at home. Meanwhile, the career woman now battles a still male-dominated work world, and is not always treated fairly. A single woman often feels she is missing the marriage experience. Conversely, the married woman often wonders what identity she has beyond being a wife. To a woman who has been married for a large portion of her life, the loss of this marriage, whatever the reasons for divorce, is devastating.

CHOICES AND LOSSES

When a marriage fails, it is a loss and we must grieve before going forward. Our identities are altered and we need to recover ourselves; it is our only choice and our only hope.

As Kenneth and Karen K. Dion observe in their essay "Romantic Love: Individual and Cultural Perspectives," love relationships suffer because in our society we confront the dilemma of being separate and independent while at the same time being expected to bend and blend as a couple. These opposed beliefs cause marital conflict, and ultimately divorce. "It is likely, for example, that the high divorce rate that characterizes American society is due in good part to the culture's exaggerated sense of individualism," they note.

When a marriage falls apart, a woman's sense of self-worth is often at an all-time low. Depending on the nature of the former marriage, a woman's self-esteem may have been plummeting for years. If a woman leaves a poor marriage, she is likely to go on to another relationship with similar characteristics because it is all she knows. A woman's confidence is shaken and despondency only worsens. Dr. Ronnie Burak advises women to be cautious. "We have the desire to return to the same kind of relationship that failed us, as if this time we can make it right," says Burak. While we do this in all sorts of connections with those close to us, for women it seems most common in love relationships.

REPETITIONS

- **Our first marriage fails because we have misunderstood our partner and ourselves**

- **We enter a new relationship, which has the same problems as the first marriage**

- **We play it out anyway, because we have low self-esteem, thus little insight**

- **Again we are divorced**

"I regret being divorced even thought my marriage wasn't the best," Phoebe, who is 46, explains. "My husband was very handsome and smart and ambitious and I bought into it. When two people couple young, as we did, it isn't ideal, but the funny part is, you think it's right—that being young and in love means it will work. There was chemistry and we had a common goal. I watched him build this business and I was there for him and the kids. I thought we were a team. My husband wanted a divorce four years ago, which shocked me and threw me into another life altogether. I know some women are okay without a husband, but I much preferred being his wife than his ex-wife.

"I have had a tough time getting over this divorce, and it is only because I am becoming realistic that I think I'll be okay. I have decided I want to be with someone who has similar interests to mine this time. I would be lying if I said that money didn't matter. Having been married to someone who has done well, I would want that again. At this stage, I don't want to help someone find clients and all of that, but I want to be with someone who is established. I am older and wiser today and in a strange way, I'm up for more challenges than I was when I was younger and thought life could only be lived by certain rules. I cannot see making another mistake. I know there won't be small children, and so the pressures of that will be over. It isn't very magical when it's a young marriage with young children. It took me a while to realize that. Finding sitters, and trying to have a life beyond the kids was not easy. I've finally lost that Cinderella expectation that a man will save me. I'll settle for a partner who is caring and I'm not thinking about his looks like I did when I was 23. Today I want someone who loves me and makes me a better person."

As women mature and have endured a divorce, they begin to look for other qualities than those they sought in the first marriage. Now a woman wants to be with someone with whom friendship can be a strong component of the union. With the discovery of someone new, comes a demand for commitment. Chemistry always counts, but might not matter as much as true intimacy and a connection not based on superficial values.

LESSONS OF DIVORCE

After a divorce, it is appropriate for a woman to reflect on what went wrong in her first marriage and what ingredients she wants in her second marriage. If nothing else, divorce teaches us to look to ourselves for answers.

The January 2001 issue of *Redbook* magazine features an exclusive with Melanie Griffith who has had three marriages, each time to an actor. Her first marriage was to Don Johnson, the second to Steven Bauer, and her present marriage is to Antonio Banderas. An example of a woman who in her forties has landed on her feet and has found the right partner, Griffith explains her philosophy: "Every woman should think of herself as a goddess. Not to be more powerful or better than anybody else, but so she can feel good about herself."

We live a long time and a relatively small portion of our married lives is focused on mothering. When the children are out of the house, we face our partners anew, and may recognize that the relationship is devoid of companionship and true caring. At this point, enough of us split up that we have to believe in a life after divorce, a new beginning. A common source of anxiety is the woman's economic state after a divorce, based on her earning power or lack thereof. Some women will take desperate measures to stave off the problem. A second marriage, in some instances, could represent a financial solution for women who have little other recourse.

The statistics on divorced women and finances are fairly

grim. Sociologist Richard R. Peterson's research on economics and divorce indicates a 27-percent income decline for women who are divorced and a 10-percent increase for men who are divorced. Alice Michaeli, sociologist, points out that a woman contributes 100 percent of her earnings—which is 77 cents for every dollar a man earns—to the marriage. After the divorce, the average husband contributes substantially less than formerly, while the woman continues to contribute 100 percent. "Single mothers and their children are the largest group of poor people in America," Michaeli remarks.

DIVORCE AND FINANCES

- **After a divorce, a woman's income declines by 27%**

- **After a divorce, a man's income increases by 10%**

- **Before a divorce, men/husbands contribute 100% of their earnings (100 cents on the dollar) to the family**

- **After the divorce, men contribute substantially less of their earnings for child support and alimony (depending on the situation)**

"When my marriage went into crisis mode," begins Kelsey, "I felt, like most women do, that I'd been neglected and that my best years had gone to the kids and to my husband without any return on my investment.

"When the kids were small, I'd made it look like a fairy-tale existence for my husband. He'd come home from work and they'd be bathed and asleep. He'd have a drink and complain about his day and I'd just listen. I never said a word. I was doing everything to make it as easy on my husband as possible. I wish I'd known at 34 what I know now. Being divorced and on my way to a new life is challenging. I think I stayed in the old life so long that by the time I put it to rest, I was ready. The walls were up and I was moving on."

Aine's story is the flip side of Kelsey's. Instead of feeling ready and prepared to leave a marriage, Aine, who is 50 today, has had a difficult time in putting her divorce behind her and in establishing the appropriate boundaries with her ex-husband. "I dated very few men after my divorce because my ex-husband was always around. He wanted us, the children and me, to be his family, and he wanted women on the side. That was the whole reason for the divorce. I did not handle the divorce well and my kids knew that it was very painful for me. So we all lived in this fantasy that it would get better, that their father would come back to us. Meanwhile, he was with another woman and then he came to me. We would have holidays together and there was this semblance of a family.

"My ex-husband was never a good provider, not in the marriage and not after the divorce. He was with a woman who made money and wanted to marry him and have children. When this ended after many years, he never closed the door on that relationship, the same way he didn't close the door on our marriage. This was his pattern and I was his victim. We were intimate off and on for years after the divorce, and then that fell apart. But he always led me to believe that he needed me somehow and I always hung in. This went on for years and created such confusion in my life. I was a divorced woman, working two jobs to support us. I was also a woman who saw a man, not in a healthy way, but a man who was my ex-husband. Finally, I learned that he was pursuing someone else, but still seeing me. It finally dawned on me that I was not the one he wanted, and that it was the same thing all over again. I had simply been there for him when he needed a home and a family. It has been devastating for me, but I have had to let go. I have to admit he is not the person I thought he was and his morals stink. It is as if I am starting over, many years after the divorce, at square one."

Sarah Blaffer Hrdy writes in her book, *Mother Nature: Maternal Instincts and How They Shape the Human Species*, that women have exchanged sexual favors for material resources in a wide range of societies, and "in societies where males control access to such resources, women commonly marry for money." A man who is a poor provider and insincere emotionally can devastate a woman. Getting over such disappointment and carving out another kind of life can be very difficult. Yet as long as we can come to terms with our reality at some point in our lives, we have a chance to redeem ourselves, and to start fresh. It takes some women much longer than necessary because they tend toward blind hope. From the start of this book, there has been an emphasis on how we are socialized and influenced by our families. It is the sum of our experiences combined with our individual natures that causes us to lead the lives we lead. When the existence is unhealthy, boundaries need to be established. Then women can go forward in a healthy manner.

BOUNDARIES AND THE EX-HUSBAND

- **Whatever occurred in the marriage, many women find themselves still trying to sort it out, and fix it**
- **Spending time with an ex-husband blurs the boundaries**
- **If one is stuck in this mode, she cannot go forward and create a new existence**
- **If boundaries are established, she can become healthy**

"Working long hours to pay for my boys was enough to make me look at my ex-husband and my past marriage for what it really was," says Barbara, who at 55 has been divorced for eight years. "Until then, I behaved as if everything was fine, as if our marriage was just like everyone else's. For a very long time, I acted like it was okay because I wanted it to be. I think back to the marriage now and I felt love for him but I was never in love with him. I knew better than that, even if I looked the other way on so many levels. But working as hard as I did, in order to keep our family together and, afterward, to keep our divided family afloat, I came to resent him.

"I think that I was too busy with work and raising the kids to consider meeting someone when I still looked good and I had more energy. It took me a long time to get over my divorce and I was down for a long time. Today the stigma seems to have lessened somewhat, but it was not easy ten years ago, when my divorce began, to be a single mother. I felt that our entire family was being judged by our church and our community. That was on top of ending one life and having to find a new one.

"As much as I struggle, I am a survivor. I have a job that works for my life right now. So much of my enthusiasm has been pushed down by the life I've led. I feel I have not lived life as I should, but I've lived for my children as a single mother. Even the job I took was based on location and not what really interested me. I did it for my kids, like everything I've done since they were born. I'm getting older now and realizing that I have to live for myself."

Divorce is a profound rejection of a partner who once selected us and with whom we planned a lifetime. This rejection, combined with the adjustment to life as a single mother and/or single woman, can be overwhelming. Lamanna and Riedmann note that, according to national surveys conducted over the past twenty years, divorced and separated people are more negative and have decreased life satisfaction. Those who are divorced also have poorer health and are more depressed than those who are married. Analysis of 6,573 responses for the National Survey of Families and Households found that even though factors such as income and education were more important, people in first marriages reported greater happiness and less depression than those who had been divorced.

DIVORCE AND MENTAL HEALTH

According to national surveys, those who are divorced are in poorer physical and mental health than married counterparts. Life satisfaction decreases, and responsibilities can be overwhelming. Those who are divorced exhibit more depression than those who are married.

The six components of divorce, as classified by the sociologist Paul Bohannan, are the emotional aspect, the legal aspect, the community aspect, the psychic aspect, the economic aspect, and the co-parenting aspect. The emotional aspect of divorce begins when the marriage is falling apart and the partners are no longer supportive of one another. Disillusionment has set in, and yet the marriage has not ended. The legal aspect is the next stage, when the divorce is actually ending through the necessary legal steps. The community aspect of divorce is what Barbara referred to in her interview, when she discussed how she felt judged by her church and her community. Friends and community change once divorce happens. Explaining to the world that one is no longer a part of a couple is not easy and some women feel demeaned by the experience. The psychic aspect of divorce involves the need for a woman to detach from her former role and see herself as a single person, a divorced woman. Lamanna and Riedmann remark that "not all divorced people fully succeed at psychic divorce... But counselors point out that this stage is a necessary prerequisite to a satisfying remarriage." The economic aspect of divorce concerns child support and alimony. Both husband and wife are now distinct economic entities.

As Brondi Borer, divorce attorney, remarks, "It is highly variable how much money of the husband's goes to his ex-wife. The court looks at all the factors, the health and age of the spouse, the ages of the children, the duration of the marriage, the number of children, before determining the alimony and child support." If the wife is the major breadwinner, there are different concerns. Co-parenting, always a big issue in divorce, concerns custody and visitation. The custodial parent assumes primary responsibility for the children, and visitation is assigned to the non-custodial parent. Joint custody is a popular form of sharing the care and responsibility for children of divorce. When divorced parents live nearby, physical custody is shared as well as decision-making.

SIX COMPONENTS OF DIVORCE

- **The Emotional Divorce**
- **The Legal Divorce**
- **The Community Divorce**
- **The Psychic Divorce**
- **The Economic Divorce**
- **The Co-parental Divorce**

Of these six components, the focus here is on the psychic and emotional divorce, which has much to do with the future of each woman's life once her divorce is finalized. The two are related because, until a woman is able to get past the anger at her former husband, and to understand what went wrong, she is not ready to acknowledge that she is separated from him and the marriage. How can a woman reclaim and reinvent herself if she doesn't truly understand herself to be in a new life, with a new identity–that of a single, divorced woman? Even if she initiated her divorce, and is pleased to terminate a stressful and untenable marriage, the adjustment period can be difficult. Women who have traditional values are liable to find their identity as divorced women more unsettling, while women who were in more egalitarian unions will not be as confused by their new status.

According to Alicia, who is 51, "The day my marriage changed, and could never change back, was the day my older daughter was born. Once our first daughter was born, my husband changed. I don't know what it was. The focus was now on this child. I don't know if it was a sense of responsibility that my husband didn't like, or if it was me, no longer being available in the same way. Maybe being there for the birth was not the best thing. Maybe it made him sick or turned him off. It felt that way. For two years I was in shock by his change of attitude. I knew my world was crumbling but I pretended it was okay–that was my facade. I was devastated inside. I felt isolated like most new mothers do. Although it was fun with the baby and I wanted a second child, it wasn't easy for me. The marriage had definitely changed.

"I couldn't believe how bad it was but I think there were

telling events along the way. Once we had a huge argument because I was sick and my husband insisted I drive upstate for him. That was when I saw how controlling he was. He wasn't there for me and would never be. I think he would have gone on with the status quo, though. But I began to see more options. I decided to go back to graduate school and to get a better job with the degree I would earn. As soon as I was on my way, I pursued my divorce. Today I am divorced, single and free. I did what was right for me and while it required courage, it was also really the only chance I had. I am not worried about being single and I am not looking for another marriage. Money will always be an issue, because my ex-husband makes more money and I know I have to support myself now and in the future. I'm working on this, and making some inroads. I tell myself that I have my children and I'm busy with my new career and my friends. This is how it is for today."

Men have traditionally had more power in a marriage since they have made more money, and in many cases been the sole breadwinners. Within certain ethnic groups this is more pronounced and expected. Yet in a marriage where both spouses work, the husband still may wield more power. The woman's career is not as important and her earnings are usually not as impressive. For those women who find themselves divorced, even with a newfound freedom, genuine concerns linger about making a living. The "marriage gradient" can leave a woman feeling stranded once she is divorced. (The "marriage gradient" concerns the difference in status when women marry above themselves and men marry below in terms of education and achievement. The concept applied more broadly at a time when women were not educated and obtained stability through their husbands' careers.)

MARRIAGE GRADIENT AND DIVORCE

When women marry a man who is superior in terms of education and career, they are marrying up. Historically men have married beneath them, because women were not as educated. If there is a divorce, these women are prepared for very little.

There are three types of marriages, as discussed by Lamanna and Riedmann in *Marriages and Families*. In a "traditional marriage" the husband has greater authority and works while his wife cares for the children and home. In a "modern marriage," husbands and wives are almost equal, but the wife's work is of less significance than her husband's. Again, the wife/mother cares for the home and children, but leisure time is devoted to the marriage. In "egalitarian marriages," which are on the rise, the spouses have equal say and influence. There is no gender delineation but an equal sharing in all areas of the relationship. If we apply the theory behind each of these kinds of marriages to women who become divorced, none of them offers solutions on the path to being single. For those divorced women who had been in a traditional marriage, the world is a more foreboding place than for those who were a modern marriage, where the wives had some kind of career and had been exposed to another realm than just homemaker. Those who were most "liberated" of all are the wives of egalitarian marriages, who seem better equipped to be single working women if their marriages do fail.

GHOSTS OF THE FIRST MARRIAGE

The more protected a woman is in her marriage, the more intimidating the outside world will be if she finds herself divorced. The skills she acquired during the marriage have a limited application to life outside of marriage.

"I have always been a freelance artist," explains Tiffany, who is 36 today. "I worked from home when the kids were small and I built up a nice little business. When my husband, who is a dentist, and I split up, I became worried about money. I thought initially during the divorce that I would get half of everything because we were divorced in an equitable distribution state. Ken, my ex-husband, became poor during the divorce, miraculously, and so I didn't get much of anything. It was a nightmare and mostly I would worry about my kids. I stayed awake at night wondering what I would do.

"I have been divorced for three years, and having had the kind of marriage where a woman seems to count, but she doesn't really count—I've had to learn a lot. I know now that no one will come to fix your broken heater when you are a single woman as fast as if you are married and a picture-perfect family. I know that cities are the only place where single mothers can feel almost equal. I learned all this the hard way. I basically knocked on doors and pushed my way in—totally outside my personality, because I had to. My divorce forced me to become more assertive and to find my place. I don't think about being single, I think about what is next and about not making the same mistake again."

Not many of us are prepared for the constancy and demands of marriage, nor are we prepared for the changes that transpire over time. Crawford and Unger note that "satisfaction often hits its slowest point when the children are school-aged or adolescents… Many couples experience the post-children stage of their marriage as a time of greater freedom and flexibility." As Katherine Rabinowitz, psychotherapist points out, "Marriages fail because once having recognized the rocky road, many people are not willing to put in the effort to smooth out the bumps. They're disillusioned, having imagined much more of a fantasy marriage. So instead of trying to work it out, either they've become so mired in the differences or so invested in being right, that it's easier to flee and try again with someone else." If a woman is acutely conscious of what her marriage entails, she is better able to work within that construct.

Becoming single does not involve the same dread and stigma as it has had in the past. The top six reasons cited by women to initiate divorce are (in order of importance): basic unhappiness, incompatibility, emotional abuse, alcohol abuse, infidelity, and physical abuse. Both men and women cite lack of communication, financial problems, sexual problems, and in-laws as causes of divorce.

WHY WOMEN SEEK DIVORCE

- **Basic unhappiness (lack of communication, financial problems, sexual problems)**
- **Incompatibility**
- **Emotional Abuse**
- **Alcohol Abuse**
- **Infidelity**
- **Physical Abuse**

"I had no problem with the word 'divorce'," Adrienne, who at 49 has been divorced for two years, remarks, "and I do not see it as a failure. It's a process, and had I been happy in my marriage, I would not have undertaken a divorce. I know many divorced women who want to be married again. I look at being divorced as an accomplishment because it wasn't something I ever anticipated doing. I was so disappointed in my marriage that I don't plan to be married again. I am with someone today and it's quite nice, but I don't need to marry him. I suppose if it became so meaningful to him to marry, I would, but it isn't something I'm planning to do, or need in my life.

"My ex-husband was from another culture and I think that had something to do with the marriage not working. We really approached things from opposite perspectives. The man I am seeing is also from another culture, but not as foreign as my husband's background. It makes a difference, and this is a little easier for me. Since I solicited my divorce and I fought hard to be independent and to take care of myself, I am not anxious to get back into a pattern which was like my marriage in any way. I know that I am more in touch with myself having left a marriage and now as a divorced woman. In a relationship it is hard to stay in touch with oneself because of the push/pull. It is sometimes hard to stand back and to see what is yours. I didn't leave my marriage looking for the next man, but for myself. My divorce taught me that I could be alone. And it made me realize that the older women get, the greater the odds are of not meeting someone. That made me face myself and be prepared for a single life. The fact that I met someone is just lucky because I learned that aloneness is lonelier than I thought. But I was prepared to do it, and ready to be single because at least it meant having myself back."

Single motherhood and pending divorce have never looked better than on Sela Ward, in her role as Lily Manning in the Lifetime television series "Once and Again." Although Lily definitely struggles to find balance between her estranged husband, Jake, the womanizer, and father to her two children, Grace and Zoe, it is her boyfriend, Rick, who gives her hope. That Rick's life is equally complicated gets this new couple through the more grueling episodes. The impressive part of the series is how authentic these characters are, and how both two single mothers in mid-life, Lily, and Rick's former wife, Karen Sammler, endeavor to make sense of their multifaceted existence.

Magazines have long called attention to famous and noto-
rious divorces. In the fall of 2000, MORE magazine did a
piece on divorcing and battling husbands and wives in midlife,
entitled "Midlife Passion." The "players" cited included Rudolph
Giuliani, the Mayor of New York City who left his wife, Donna
Hanover, for Judith Nathan, his current companion. In good
company were Jane Fonda, who is described as having fore-
gone her career for the now-soured marriage with Ted Turner,
and Anna Wintour, the editor of *Vogue*, who fell in love with
"Texas cell-phone millionaire Shelby Bryan." Both left their
spouses to become a couple.

Passion is not always the incentive for divorce and a new
lease on life. Alison Spear, who was written up in the September 2000 issue of *Vogue* in an article entitled "Suddenly Single,"
talks about how her jewelry was repossessed by the United
States Government when her then-husband, Carlos Gomez,
was indicted. Soon after, it seems, she and Gomez were no
long married. In a very upbeat manner, Spear, an architect and
single mother, discusses how easy it was to discard the jewelry
that was confiscated by the FBI. Apropos of parting with prized
possessions, the article has a brief mention of Marla Maples,
Donald Trump's second ex-wife, and her sale of his engagement ring to her at auction for $110,000. The moral of the
story is that marriage does not always last and neither do the
stones that go with the marriage. "In the past," David Anicich,
director of sales at Verdura, is quoted in the article as saying,
"the husband came in and purchased jewelry that showed off
a certain level of success. *His* success. Today, women are actually choosing jewelry that they will enjoy and wear, not just

showcasing their husbands' financial position." Spear, as a representative of divorced and independent women, is quoted as saying, "My ex-husband didn't have my taste anyway."

The media's recent message is that we can survive divorce easily and glibly enter singledom, as divorced women–not to be confused with never-married single women. Never-married single women have a different approach to their status, and are perceived by society differently. Recent literature and media interpretation of the never-married woman are upbeat. And while on the popular television series "Friends" single women are in search of the ideal mate, they also have a bountiful single existence. This was true for "Seinfeld" too, where single life may have been idiosyncratic and quirky, but a support system of friends filled the voids.

A *New York Times* article published on October 29th, 2000 by Shaila K. Dewan, entitled "Call Me Miss (and Fabulous and Single)" explored the mind-set of single women in their thirties in terms of how they wish to be addressed. Being called "Miss" if single, or "Mrs." if married, became politically incorrect in the 1970s. "Ms." became the only acceptable title for women, married or not, at that time. "Although one survey found that by the early 1980s a third of American women supported the use of Ms., there was still substantial resistance," writes Dewan. So while "Ms." eventually met with widespread acceptance by the mid-eighties, women in their late twenties and early thirties today eschew it and prefer "Miss." The advantage for a single woman in using "Miss," according to Dewan, is that "it lets people know you are eligible, but stops short of suggesting that you're available."

Contrary to popular belief, the "old maid" is not someone to be pitied or stereotyped. According to Mary Crawford and Rhoda Unger, those women who have never married are physically healthier and enjoy better economic resources than their married counterparts. In many cases, these women are single by choice and have a rich social life and extended family life. Perhaps the well-adjusted, contented single woman can be a role model for the newly single, divorced woman who carries tremendous emotional baggage from her years of marriage in her foray into the single world. Her identity has been invested in marriage and family, while a never-married single woman has not known this. Both types of single women might want to find a partner; some might want to marry. Others will build a life for themselves that resonates with friendships, relationships with co-workers, and family. These women often feel more complete than their married or divorced counterparts.

SINGLE BY CHOICE

Those women who are never married have a unique attitude about their lives. They have developed a life that is complete without a partner.

vs. DIVORCED WOMEN

Women who have initiated the divorce are more positive and confident of their new role as divorced women than those who did not wish to divorce. In both cases, these women have to adjust their identity.

Author Gail Sheehy in her book, *New Passages: Mapping Your Life Over Time*, touches on the fact that in the past twenty years women between the ages of 45 and 54 are now opting to remain single more than divorced men. This is affirmative for women because it represents choice. The choice, in this case, is to create a life that they control because it is theirs.

"I don't intend to be alone for the rest of my days," says Cecelia, who at 41, was married for eighteen years and divorced this year, "but I also am enjoying it for the time being. For years I had to concentrate on my husband and the house. I felt like I was far away from myself for years and I am finally feeling like I can think about me. I was treated very badly in my marriage and it has taken me a long time to get over it. If I didn't have a good job and my sisters, I don't know how I would have gotten through. I watched some of my friends divorce and remarry and I never wanted that. I was jealous of their divorces, but not of their new marriages. For me it was so hard to get divorced that I couldn't think much beyond it.

"I had been married young and I never really had the chance to be single. There is a universe I know nothing about and I am ready to learn. I am getting myself in order, and I am trying to look good and feel better. I was so miserable in my marriage that I became angry and ugly. Now I am looking like myself again. I try not to ask myself questions like who would want me. Instead I ask myself who I would want."

When women feel disillusioned after a divorce, they are often frightened by life outside the bounds of marriage, even if they desire to be unmarried. As women age, they feel unmarketable, thanks to media hype and our culture's fascination with youth. Being single offers an opportunity for women to stretch psychically and spiritually so that their personal development soars. Divorce and singledom affect women differently at various stages in their lives. While some women might become frustrated in their attempts to find the right partner, and decide to create a fulfilling life as a single woman, others will push on with the search. If a woman's expectations in a new mate are unrealistic, it will feel hopeless and futile. For a woman who has the right approach to her divorce and being on her own, there are many possibilities.

Becoming a single, divorced woman is a strenuous journey, regardless of the circumstances that surround the breakup. It is only when we have clarity about ourselves, when we are certain why we have left our marriage and what our mission is in the next stage of our life, that we can succeed in our pursuit.

6

Reinvention / Remarriage

"Today I am remarried to an older, successful man," Amy, at 44, begins, "and it is so unlike my first marriage. I married this man because he gives me a life I am ready to have now. But what happened to me here was totally unanticipated. He is not really wealthy and not one bit generous. I was very surprised by his lack of generosity. One of the reasons that I chose him was for his lifestyle. I thought that if I couldn't have children, I would have a lifestyle that I enjoyed. Instead I have learned that I still have to work—which I like, but did not anticipate having to do. And because our society teaches that women are to be cared for by men, it is hard to accept that men do not pay for everything. In a strange way this marriage has fostered an independence I never expected. I have created my own stock portfolio all in my name and I no longer expect him to be giving me large gifts or small.

"I think back to my first marriage, when I was too young and naive to appreciate anything. The potential to blend what was mine with what was his was definitely there. This marriage is about practicality. Whatever I imagined to be romantic about marriage has gone by the wayside. I look at this like a business proposition of sorts. And I have adapted to his way of thinking because I needed to in order to make a success of it."

In my research for *Second Wives*, I learned that three out of four women remarry after their divorce and four out of ten marriages involve a second marriage for one of the partners. While the hope is that the answer lies in the new marriage, there are always complications from the past, such as stepchildren and former spouses. For many women however, remarriage represents the completion of a course of action. This began with divorce, followed by an unfamiliar period as a single, a newfound independence–culminating in a new beginning, in a love relationship based on the commitment that marriage entails. With the notion of marriage so firmly ingrained in our society, once it dissolves there are many who are ready for the next, with the hope that this one will do the trick. And if not the second time, perhaps the third.

REMARRIAGE AND REDISCOVERY

Women look to the next marriage once the first has failed. Despite the damage of a previous marriage, there is usually hope in trying again and getting it right.

There are those who have made a career of remarrying, such

as Elizabeth Taylor, who has been married eight times. If our society has encouraged us to ensnare a man once, why not twice—or as many times as necessary to get it right? Yet studies show, as sociologist Jessie Bernard noted in the early 1970s, that marriage benefits men more than women and married men live longer than those who are not married. While this result has been discussed and reiterated and is supposedly a known fact, it tends not to be taken seriously. The desire to be married again, after a failed marriage, still matters very much to a large population of women. And of course, romantic love can still be a factor, in addition to all the more pragmatic attractions of remarriage.

Jungian Psychoanalyst Clarissa Pinkola Estes, Ph.D., likens the beginning of a relationship to "The Accidental Finding of Treasure" in her book "Women Who Run With Wolves." Estes describes seven tasks "that teach one soul to love another deeply and well." These include: the discovery of the other person as a spiritual treasure, understanding the "Life/Death/Life" parts of a relationship, trusting the person and being able to share "both future dreams and past sadness." The latter seems to apply particularly to second marriages, where both parties have endured disappointments and are ready to begin a new life together, recognizing full well what can go awry in love and marriage.

"My second marriage is all about loving each other," Elsa, at 40, tells us. "Whatever was missing from my first marriage is in the second. I think this is a combination of being with the right person, having gone through a bad marriage so that I really appreciate this one, and realizing who I am. It takes guts to leave a marriage with kids, without anyone waiting in the wings. I might not have done it if I hadn't gone to a college reunion. I looked around the room, and I realized how old we all looked because we were–this was my fifteenth reunion. That was what started it for me. I saw an old boyfriend and it made me very sad. He seemed so happy with his life. Later I learned that he wasn't, because so few people really are.

"A year after that reunion, I decided I wanted a divorce. I'd thought about it a lot, but I believed that this was my fate, to have these darling children and this husband who I couldn't relate to. Things got worse and I thought about how young I'd once been. I was divorced within eighteen months. I didn't go out at first, because I wanted to prepare myself for the world. I was in shock. The year after my divorce was worse for me than the year it was happening. Finally I thought I was ready, and I was fixed up by some friends. That is how I met my husband. It's been dreamy and at the same time very realistic. I never pretended anything, nor did he. We both come with a lot of baggage, and we have always acknowledged it. I took a long hard look at life and at myself by being divorced and being single. Remarriage was not a leap of faith for me, because I married the right person, and I finally knew what I wanted for myself."

Women between the ages of 30 and 40 are better able to recuperate from a poor marriage and remarry with the right intentions. In contrast, the babyboomers, whose fantasy of an idyllic married life dies hard, tend to hold on longer to what is not right for them in the first marriage. Once that has ended, this population is inclined to suffer more than the generation behind them. They are crushed by their failed marriages. The awakening is not easy for this group, and regaining their health and inner balance is a formidable task. Unless they come to terms with their past and what their needs are, they are in danger of making another mistake in a new marriage.

WOMEN 30 to 40

These women are better equipped to leave a poor marriage and to find the right partner in a remarriage. If they have lost their way, the journey back is possible.

vs.

FEMALE BABYBOOMERS

These women have put great stock in their marriages. When they fail, they cannot easily heal, nor can they readily collect themselves and move on.

While there is no way to recapture lost opportunities in our lives or years gone by, it is quite possible—and valuable—to understand our errors of the past. One of the greatest mistakes in a second marriage occurs when the parties do not know what went wrong in the first. Unless the past is put to rest, it will come between partners in the remarriage. It is almost as if the partners are fungible and the drama is what persists. There are many emotions associated with divorce that can spill over to the new marriage, if we have not evolved and grown from the process. Anger, regret, lack of boundaries, residual pain, can come into play with sad consequences. "A common experience for divorced women, even if they are relieved about the divorce and planning a new marriage, is that they feel cheated," says Brondi Borer, divorce attorney. "These women have had husbands and children, and have denied their sacrifices and discontent for years. Then they reach their forties and become divorced. These women can never be 30 or 35 again, in any part of their lives. Those who do best are the ones who figure out a way to make a new life, and remarriage is a big part of it."

Self magazine published an article by Pamela Redmond Satran in November 2000, called "Are you getting in your own way?" Several of the questions asked apply to our patterns in new relationships. For example, "If they don't call, do you assume they don't want you?" "In life and in love, do you ask for what you know you can get as opposed to what you really want?" And, "Do you find you've got a lot more enthusiasm at the beginning of projects than you do in the middle?" The answer sheet indicates that if one answers positively to more than six of the questions, she is a self-sabotager. The last thing a woman wants after a failed first marriage is a failed second one. There is little that could eat away at one's self-esteem and personal courage more than such an experience. And so, as repetitious as it is, I must underscore that unless a woman is ready to go forward and has had a personal evolution, the same issues will recur. It may not be a deliberate action, but its resonance will be very strong.

"I was so angry in my first marriage," Antonia, at 43, admits, "that I let it spill over to the second marriage. I was married to a man whose family disregarded me and treated me like dirt. I lost touch with my family because I moved half way across the country to be with my husband. I hung on tightly to my brother who lived nearby and to my friends as a way to get through. There were problems with my youngest child and that also kept me there for longer than I wanted. I suppose that women always make excuses and stay in bad marriages. But my family was so far away and I didn't have the strength to leave. By the time I divorced I was ready to go.

"Then I met someone who seemed different but I now know is very much the same as my first husband. The difference is me. I see this person in another light. I am more established too, in my work–which I had to be once I was divorced–and I am more realistic about my life. This husband would also ask me to give up too much of myself, but I know better than to do it again. Instead, I deal with him, and since I've changed, it is not the same relationship as in my first marriage. Maybe I'm here, in this marriage, because I don't want to be alone like I was after my divorce. Maybe I do it because I'm beyond young children, I'm beyond needing a husband to make money, and now there is a chance at just having a union–flawed as it is."

"Women will remain in bad first marriages and bad second marriages for the same reason," Dr. Michaele Goodman notes, "because they are afraid of being alone. In order to leave a bad marriage a woman must overcome her fear of being unwanted. She has to have the idea that she could meet someone even if no one is waiting. She has to feel desirable." As social attitudes have changed toward divorce and remarriage, women, even those of us who are "nice girls" who never imagined being positioned as married/divorced/remarried, are being bolder about taking the initiatives necessary to get there. Remarriage may not be the pursuit and objective for every divorced woman, but of my interviewees, there were more who looked to a fresh, permanent relationship than those who did not–by a ratio of four to one.

PERPETUAL DREAM

After the dream of being a perfect bride to a perfect man shatters, the new dream emerges. The flawed bride to a flawed husband appears, conscious of their respective limitations and, hopefully, shatterproof.

There are no fairy tales about midlife brides, divorcées who have triumphed and are now looking for a second chance at happiness. And there might never be, since our daughters, although we have high hopes for them in terms of their choices, are still raised on Snow White and Sleeping Beauty. It is ironic that when in 2000 the television industry put its latter-day spin on a traditional fairy tale, it backfired severely. The show, "How to Marry a Millionaire," arranged a story-book wedding between midlife strangers (with the groom allowed to choose his bride much like a Miss America pageant). It fell apart when the bride, Darva Conger, would not consummate the marriage on the prearranged honeymoon, and Rick Rockwell, the groom, was revealed to have a questionable reputation in both his private and professional life. That a network could have so sorely lost on such a hopeful theme is inexplicable. The viewers were intrigued, because the illusion of marriage, romance, and an affluent life is so ingrained in our culture. The latest bride magazine, *Bride Again,* which features brides who have married before and dare to call themselves "brides," is further proof that females in our society are geared toward marriage, with the adage holding strong–if at first you don't succeed, try, try again.

When Jacqueline Bouvier Kennedy married Aristotle Onassis in 1968, five years after she was widowed, it was a remarriage for both parties. The world watched agape at this union which seemed a fairy-tale marriage of a whole other order than Jackie's first marriage, which was her entrance into the American "Camelot." The marriage to Onassis was filled with riches, yachts, and had a distinctively European flavor. Both partners had children from their previous marriages and obligations to their first families. While Jackie had been deeply identified with the American dream, Onassis was not American but Greek. It is sheer speculation whether or not the late Princess Diana, had she lived, would have married Dodi El-Fayed, her beau at the time of her death. This too would have been a departure from her first marriage, and like Mrs. Onassis' second marriage, would have had a more European and a less political character.

The majority of women I interviewed reported that their new marriages were unlike their old ones. This came with concerted effort and the determination to get it right the second time around. This group also found that their divorces and time put in as single women prepared them for remarriage. In the first marriage, many times the wives accommodated their husbands and children, while in the remarriage a more egalitarian model of marriage, as described in the previous chapter, asserts itself. The new marriage, ideally, should blend the lessons of the past with the ambitions of the future. While wives are often resentful and torn in their marital roles in the first marriage, the second marriage offers security and autonomy. Not raising children together actually creates a relationship that emphasizes the couple rather than the children. There is not a mother I have spoken to who does not recognize that having children impacts the marriage and forever redefines the dynamic between husband and wife.

As Elizabeth L. Paul notes in her essay "Midlife Interpersonal Relationships," there are five relationship areas that matter for women in midlife. These include contact with friends and one's spouse, and connection to one's children, siblings, and mothers. Women are deeply invested in these relationships at this stage in their lives, and any conflict in these relationships is disturbing.

PERKS IN LATER-LIFE MARRIAGE

The remarriage becomes the main relationship for women in midlife. The children are grown and friendships have long been established. Women are better equipped to be sensitive to their husband's needs and vice versa.

Two important elements of remarriage are sexuality and

spirituality. Women who have survived a first marriage have often expressed initial dismay–or relief–when sex disappeared from the equation. Once children are born, and the pressures of daily life build up, sex soon gets slighted. It doesn't get easier for a couple as their children get older, in terms of intimacy and having time for sex and romance in the marriage. Shere Hite's survey reports that a majority of women feel that their teenage children add stress to the marriage, and 68 percent view their children as having detracted from the marriage and from time with their husbands.

Women have expressed a renewed interest in sex when they remarry. Wives report a revived sense of confidence and fulfillment in their relations with their husbands. While the visits from stepchildren may inhibit the sex somewhat, the overall rhythm is one that has a special place in the marriage. This remains one component of a healthy, positive marriage.

"In this marriage," Callie says, smiling, "I wanted someone who loves me as much as I love him. Having had two unhappy marriages, I did not want to convince myself of anything this time. Over the years, I had stuck it out in two relationships without any real intimacy or caring. The first time I knew something was missing and I got divorced, and the second time I couldn't believe it was happening again, nor could I face it, so I stayed and missed what I needed. Instead of admitting how much was not there, both times I stayed, miserably. I really expected the second marriage to be close, joyful, and fun. It hadn't been like that.

"When I met Mark, I knew I didn't have to be stubborn and prove to the world that he was okay–he was okay, for real.

I had learned to listen, and I listened when he told me about himself and his values. I was careful this time, because in my last marriage, my ex-husband made excuses for everything–it was always someone else's fault. Mark had none of this shtick, and that gave me hope. I don't have to be in denial here, I can be open and honest and it works. The sex and intimacy take me to a place I've never been before–it's a reflection of our feelings for each other. Part of my problem had been that I always imagined my life to be picture-perfect, like on TV, with nice kids and a smiling husband. I finally found the smiling husband."

TRUST AND SECURITY

When the partners are secure in the marriage, they can trust each other and their feelings. The intimacy is genuine, and the relationship becomes more profound.

An excellent illustration of a lasting marriage bond, where the original marriage almost evolves into a remarriage, is represented by the myth of Odysseus and Penelope, his long-suffering wife. Odysseus and Penelope were joint rulers of Ithaca when the Trojan War broke out and he was called to battle and reluctantly acquiesced. The war lasted for ten years and the trip home to Ithaca lasted another ten, with seductions and obstacles along the way. Penelope was also tested, by suitors who wanted her kingdom. Her resistance took the form of weaving a funeral shroud for her father-in-law that took her twenty years to complete and kept her suitors at bay. It was the faith which Odysseus and Penelope shared that sustained their hope for two decades and resulted in a renewed marriage in the end.

The spiritual side of remarriage enhances the union for both wife and husband. Faith in one's partner and faith in oneself are the most valuable factors in a meaningful love relationship, and hopefully the basis of a remarriage. Judith Orloff writes in her book, *Intuitive Healing: 5 Steps to Physical, Emotional, and Sexual Wellness*: "A relationship is never just about two people. It's also infused with a spiritual force." Orloff speaks of "being mirrors for each other," such that in a marriage or a close relationship we are the emotional mirror for our partner. This works for both positive and negative feedback, and can strengthen the relationship. Thomas More in his book *Soul Mates* encourages us to "care for the soul of a marriage," and warns against partners who will "blame each other for not living up to promises made at the time of their wedding or engagement." More suggests that we "honor a marriage's soul by discovering what it wants," whether it be distance, closeness, or a lifelong commitment. What is important is that we are able to recognize our own marriage for its specific traits and inner workings and to honor the marriage on that basis. Again, the potential for this level of reflectiveness is enhanced in remarriage.

HONORING THE NEW MARRIAGE

- **As individuals we have come to understand ourselves and our needs**

- **We bring our self-knowledge to the new marriage**
- **The marriage has its own soul and requirements**

"After my first marriage, where I was a doormat, I was not prepared to do that again," Raquel, at 44, describes her situation. "I decided to retrieve myself and listen to my inner voice before I went out and got involved with anyone. I took a long hard look at myself and listed what my ultimate goals were. By the time I met Seth, I had made decisions for myself and how I wanted to conduct my life. I did not intend to give up my own needs for the benefit of a relationship. And he understood that and listened to me.

"Together we built a very specific kind of world. The 'soul' of our marriage is about how much we care, and about how separate we are, yet together. I do not believe that a couple has to have the same interests—say, loving a sport or some kind of hobby. But the values have to be the same. And there has to be some kind of connection. It can't be contrived—it has to really exist. This marriage goes beyond my expectations—it has a life of its own. I wonder if I ever would have recognized its worth if I hadn't been in such a bad place first."

Although the spiritual nature of a remarriage is uplifting and promising, one cannot avoid the stark realities of this union. In *Second Wives: The Pitfalls and Rewards of Marrying Widowers and Divorced Men*, I discuss the most common problems in second marriages, which can be applied to third and fourth marriages as well. They are finances, stepchildren, and the unfinished business of the past. Unfinished business means the husband or wife has not resolved the original fit of his or her prior marriage, and so it is brought into the new marriage. My research indicated that unless boundaries are established when it comes to stepchildren and the expectations are laid out carefully, this will be a point of contention for the couple. Finances should be treated in the same way, with full guidelines and disclosure.

Yet, as we know, in these new marriages, even the best-laid plans can go unrealized since we bring so much baggage to the relationship. In other words, a remarriage can begin with the husband and his wife living in California and the stepchildren living across the country. Suddenly a 16-year-old stepson comes to live with his father, or a 25-year-old stepdaughter breaks up with her boyfriend and comes home to live.

There are surprises when it comes to finances and remarriage as well. All is well if a husband has a great job and is paying his child support and alimony, but if he loses his job it creates pressure in the marriage. There are some wives with terrific jobs who unexpectedly find themselves subsidizing their husband's former family in these instances. In actuality, both partners enter the marriage with their own responsibilities—those of children, elderly parents, mortgage payments. Patricia Schiff Estess, author of *Money Advice for Your Successful Remarriage*, recommends methods of avoid co-mingling the new marital wealth in this circumstance by taking out a home equity loan. Although the distinctions do fade over the years, this is a way of avoiding resentment over money matters.

"From an emotional and psychological standpoint," Ms. Estess explains, "most women who have been divorced feel they've been burned financially. Statistically this is true, since women do more poorly than men in a divorce. Now these women become more conscious of the decision-making process in the remarriage. They have lived on their own and are more sophisticated and have developed a style of handling money. Their husbands also have a style of their own, and so one of the things to consider is how to join money. Most women feel comfortable having their own account and a joint account at the same time. This exhibits a certain amount of independence and control over money and still shows the family—however it is configured—that as a unit they are valued too."

FINANCIAL SOLUTIONS

Divorced women have been hurt financially. They then develop their own savvy when it comes to money. It is wise for them in the remarriage to keep their own account independent of their husband's.

Amy Reisen, divorce attorney, cites money as commonly one of the biggest issues in divorce and remarriage. "There are those women who, when they become divorced, have no marketplace skills," says Reisen. "Even if they had an interest twenty years ago, it has long since been abandoned. This is a real problem if there is not enough money to go around and no financial cushion or money put away. Couples who have been counting on an annuity or a pension plan now have to support two houses. The judge looks at what the husband's obligation is to his kid and his ex-spouse and this becomes spousal and child support. If a judge has to decide between college tuition for his child and spousal support, he may favor the tuition over the support. This is very rough on the women, and it creates a problem for them in the future unless they get out there and work. These ex-wives could remarry, and have another husband support them, or the ex-husband could remarry and continue to pay spousal support/alimony for a long time."

BAGGAGE FROM THE PAST

What husbands bring to new marriage:

- **A financial obligation to his children**
- **A financial obligation to the former wife**
- **Two homes to support**
- **College tuition/s**

What wives bring to new marriage:

- **Lack of marketable skills to land a job**
- **Lack of spousal support**
- **Gap between child support payments and costs for children**

As in any honest relationship–which is the aim–there needs to be a serious discussion about both partners' situation and an assessment of what will suffice in each instance. Deborah, who was divorced at the age of 40 with four children, had alimony and child support in place until she remarried, three years later. Today, she believes that not enough provisions were made for these circumstances.

"When my divorce came through," Deborah remembers, "I thought it was fine and that I was set financially. I'd been married for thirteen years and I was entitled to alimony which was intended to get me back on my feet. My children were all in public school and I figured I was okay. I took a part-time job in an office not too far from the house and had custody of the kids. A year later I unexpectedly met a man who I fell in love with and he became my husband a year later. I love him so much and we have a wonderful marriage, but money issues and kids always add some tension to an otherwise perfect setup. I lost my alimony when I got married again, which was expected. Then my second-oldest child wanted to go to a special dance school, which is private. And it's a great opportunity for her, but it had to come half out of my pocket. Then my job became full time, but the money I make doesn't really justify having to pay a sitter for the younger kids, so that's another expense. My ex-husband has been pleading poor for the last year, and I doubt it's true. But he says he can't pay for college next year. And my son is staying at his dad's more, and so my ex-husband is also cutting back on child support for him, because of this. I don't want to take him to court on it, but it is so tight with the money.

"I thought that my husband and I talked about anything

and everything that could happen before we married. He has one child, who lives abroad right now, so he has none of this. I really feel like the rug has been pulled out from under me, and the financial support I thought I could count on is getting smaller."

In contrast with Deborah's position, Lucia made every provision she could with her ex-husband at the suggestion of her present husband. "I had the advantage of knowing my present husband during my divorce. I met him at the beginning and he helped me as a friend for the first few months before we began to date. He suggested that my lawyer cover any possible scenario so that I wouldn't get screwed. My divorce stipulates that even if one of my two girls goes to live with their father, I still get the same amount of money for that child. And I put off my marriage to Rick for one year because I really needed the alimony payments for those months. Then I decided it was ridiculous and said to myself, Don't be one of those women, get on with your life.

"The strangest part about being remarried is that I am always aware of my past through not only the children, but through those child-support checks that I count on. Had I been divorced in certain states, my child support would only last until the kids are 18. In this state, it is 21. That makes a huge difference. I don't want Rick to see me sweating it out over the kids, but I already know that once those payments stop, I'll still be paying for stuff for my girls. What can I do—they're my children. The one thing Rick insisted I had in the agreement was that their father would pay for college and even for their weddings. Although I don't ever want to ask Rick, if I did, I know he would help me out with something for the girls. And he would look at it that way, as helping the girls, not their father."

Not only are finances an issue in remarriage, but finances almost always concern the stepchildren. If one marries a man who has these obligations, or if a man marries a woman with children and child support, it cannot be wished away. The first wife and first family will not somehow mystically disappear just because there is a remarriage. Financial obligations and stepchildren are here to stay. A better approach is to create the marriage as a partnership and work on the obstacles together.

Stepchildren are the other issue in remarriage, as mentioned above, and volumes have been written about this topic. According to the SAA Families of the 21st Century (formerly the Stepfamily Association of America), 65 percent of remarriages involve children from a prior marriage. Twenty-three percent of the children live only with their biological mother in the U.S. today. Our society behaves as if stepfamilies can be similar to nuclear families, when in fact they cannot. The harsh reality for children of divorce is that their former family is gone, replaced with a stepfamily if a remarriage takes place. The new spouses, however, often enter the remarriage with an idealized vision of the new "family"—a replica of the Brady Bunch. If the partners in the remarriage are not prepared for the challenges and obstacles of a stepfamily, they will find it a shock to their system and their dreams may quickly be shattered.

STEPCHILDREN AND REMARRIAGE

- **65% of remarriages involve children from a prior marriage**
- **23% of children live with a single mother today**
- **A stepfamily does not replace an intact family**
- **There are repercussions for the children**

According to Dr. Marjorie Engel, President of SAA Families of the 21st Century (formerly the Stepfamily Association of America), when at least one of the new partners brings a child or children from a prior relationship to the remarriage, this constitutes a stepfamily. "Stepfamilies are not 'blended' families," says Dr. Engel, "because the expectation of 'blending' is getting rid of family relationships that previously existed and creating a replacement. The concept of 'blending' negates the past and makes the present more difficult to manage. Families join together, families combine, but they do not 'blend.' Successful stepfamilies have learned how to respect the past by recognizing and supporting the need and right of children to share in the lives of all their parents and other relatives while they build a stepfamily future together."

"I worry about my children and the time they spend with their father and his new wife," says Tina, who at 41 has been divorced for six years and remarried for two. "And I feel sad when the kids are not nice to my husband, Howard. His kids are younger, and boys, which somehow makes it easier. My children are older and can be difficult. But my image of getting married again included having a happy stepfamily, with the kids all gathered around for holidays. I guess I thought that because I love Howard, my kids would love him. It isn't so. Meanwhile, they are quite seduced by my ex-husband and his new wife. She has bought the kids, literally. Every other weekend they come home with bags full of new clothes and CDs. I find it upsetting and off-putting. I don't want to compete, and yet I feel there are constant comparisons being made between the two homes. The values I have instilled in my children no longer seem to have any weight. This, plus the fact that we are not a 'happy stepfamily' makes it all so discouraging for me.

"My brother is divorced and remarried to a woman who adores his kids. She has two children and they live with them. His children come on weekends. Everyone seems to get along and they do things as a family. I'm so sorry that it hasn't worked out this way for us. I can't really figure out what we've done so differently that it hasn't happened."

In *Divorce and New Beginnings* author Genevieve Clapp, Ph.D. discusses the myths of stepfamilies and those unrealistic expectations of a remarriage with children. The myths are the following: that remarriage gets people back on their feet after divorce, that there is an instant family after the remarriage, that once the marriage takes place there will be a traditional family again, and that there is merely a brief adjustment period for the stepfamily. As Tina's story indicates, the hope that all will be well and flow smoothly is too seldom realized. Women in remarriages and stepfamilies are in for some trying times. The children on one or both sides are usually uncooperative. There could be pressure from the ex-spouse and his significant other, and two separate homes with separate rules and standards are trying for the children. The marriage is strained by these circumstances. Few couples are prepared for what transpires with stepchildren as they build the foundation for their new life together. For women who are true romantics, the idealism of a new happy stepfamily blurs the reality. Women would do better to pay close attention to what transpires between the children and stepparents.

COMPLICATIONS AND LOW BLOWS

The unrealistic hopes in a remarriage with children disintegrate in the harsh light of day. The children from both sides can be uncooperative and act out. The disparate styles of the two households for children of divorce are pronounced in remarriages. The parents/newlyweds are baffled and ill-equipped for their children's attitudes.

"I would not let my daughters' feelings about Craig stop me," says Beatrice, a 36-year-old divorced mother who is presently engaged. "I had a terrible first marriage and this new marriage promises me great things. My girls liked him in the beginning and once it became serious, they started to find fault with him. The worst part is that Craig is not really up for their fight. He has kids of his own so it isn't like he doesn't know children. And he has tried everything, but I can tell that he is getting tired of it all. I let the girls know that I am entitled to some happiness, but that means little to them. They are adolescent and don't care about my needs.

"I feel that I am being undermined by their father, who does not want me to marry again. He is married, so it surprises me that he feels this way. After the girls' behavior toward Craig, which threw me for a loop, their father's influence was the next big shock. I guess I thought I had it all figured out, that we would buy this big old house and all the kids would have rooms of their own. But it isn't enough. Nothing would be enough. That's what I have learned. So I'm just going to be selfish and marry him, because I want to be his wife. We'll get through the rest, somehow."

If we are in touch with ourselves, if we are able to self-actualize, and to take what happened in the past and put it to good use, then we will be ready to move on. It is only when a woman has done some soul-searching and has had enough distance from her marriage to let go of the anger and learn from her past, that she will be ready for her next marriage, if remarriage is what she wants.

What makes the remarriage successful is the commitment that the two partners have to one another. The deterrents and stumbling blocks are obvious, yet the incentive is there too. Since remarriage comes after a struggle to readjust, it is a great fortune to find someone with whom we want to share the rest of our life. The key in remarriage, as in the other steps we take in reclaiming ourselves, is that we be wide-awake in the process. This is in order to get it right and, above all, to achieve happiness and equanimity in our choice.

7

Mothering: Choices In and Out of Reality

"I always knew I wanted to have a child," begins Maryanne, who at 52 is a single mother. "In my thirties I had been with someone and we talked about getting married. It was a rocky relationship and I was committed but I also knew I wanted a child. I was having trouble conceiving and he made it more difficult. Then I had a miscarriage and we finally broke up. Although I knew it had been no good, I still wanted to be a mother and I did not want to miss this piece of my life. Some important years had passed in terms of fertility and there was nothing to be done about that.

"I began dating a man soon after and his impression of me was that I was driven by my career. I am an attorney in a very male-dominated law firm and it is true that this had been a motivating force for much of my life. But I had also been preoccupied with becoming a mother, with having a baby. While I was seeing this man, I accidentally became pregnant. That was when I had to face it. I was close to 40 and I made the choice because had I had an abortion, I would never have a child. When I told him, I made an offer. I said that if he wanted to participate in raising this child, he could, because I was determined to have this baby. He wanted no part of it and I raised the child by myself. I don't know if I could have gone to a sperm bank, the identity of the father meant something to me. My parents were very supportive and I felt strongly that I had made the right decision.

"I was an anomaly thirteen years ago, and not many women were doing what I did, having babies without fathers and raising them by themselves. People were judgmental about me and my choice. In a strange way it helped me to see the world as it is—I began to judge it, too. I was also lucky because I had a child without having a poor marriage, I didn't have to stay in an unhappy union for the sake of the child. But having my daughter is about me—about me as a woman and a mother."

While our mothering instincts may be very strong, they are reinforced by the significance society attaches to motherhood. The implicit message for women is that if they are not mothers, they have not achieved complete satisfaction and are lacking something essential in their lives. The stereotypical role and expectations of motherhood persist, despite the increase in choices for women—in the workplace, in terms of marrying or not marrying, as working mothers versus traditional non-working mothers. Although children are prized in this society and many women long to have them, the payoff in terms of happiness is ambiguous. Just as surveys indicate that unmarried women are actually happier than married women, so many studies show that women with children have a lower life satisfaction and lower marriage satisfaction than those without. And yet, women have been raised to believe that this is our primary responsibility to ourselves–to be responsible, nurturing mothers. There is a preconceived notion that women were born to marry and have children, and that their altruism is all-inclusive. Our dedication to our children is supposedly our fondest wish and greatest obligation. Anything less is failure, regardless of our other accomplishments.

MOTHERHOOD AS ORDAINED

- **Our society dictates motherhood for women**
- **It has been idealized since we were small girls**
- **However else we have configured our life, it is hollow without the mothering experience**

Within our cultural tradition mothers are expected to assume primary responsibility for child rearing, whether they work or not. Tradition stipulates that mothers make themselves more available to children, while fathers who work are not available on the same basis. According to the Peterson's 1997 study, 47 percent of mothers felt they did not have enough support from their husbands when it came to parenting.

A *Wall Street Journal* article on October 13, 2000 revealed how far-reaching the desire for motherhood is, even today. Nancy Keates writes in "The Ultimate 40th-Birthday Gift" that women who have children nearing adolescence are now beginning over with diapers. The percentage of women giving birth between the ages of 40 and 44 is up 23 percent in the past six years. Since women have started families later in life, becoming a mom when you're 40 or over makes sense. Another factor in continuing to have babies is the desire to stay young, to prove one's fertility. Financially these families tend to be sound, and the wives/mothers have often given up an impressive career for mothering. Because these mothers did it late in the game, as a conscious choice, often after many attempts, they tend to be less regretful, more grateful and content. According to Keates, experts in the field view delayed parenting as a bonus for the children since older mothers make better mothers.

In the U.S., between 1970 and 1987, the number of women who waited until their thirties to have their first child increased 400 percent. More than half of all women in their early thirties who don't have a child yet are still planning to someday. The birth rates for women between 40 and 44 are also higher in the last fifteen years. This postponement seems to benefit the mother emotionally; the woman who has a child in her early twenties may come to resent "the best years of her life" which she devoted to parenting, and feel unfulfilled.

LATER MARRIAGES/OLDER MOTHERS

- **Women who become mothers in their**

twenties account for 52% of the population

- **In the last twenty-five years, the birth rates for women in their thirties and forties has steadily risen**

- **Older prospective mothers face the challenges of infertility**

"I had my first child at 24," Marsha tells us. "Today, at the age of 43, I have four children, and the youngest is twelve. By the time I was pregnant with him, I was within the normal range to be having a baby. The first three brought down the average of those expecting mothers sitting in the OB/GYN's office. And I was always the youngest mother in every grade. Now I see it as an advantage, but for the first two children in particular, I was growing up with them. I didn't feel like their mother, I felt like their babysitter. And the worst part was that I kept thinking I was missing life. So while I loved them dearly from the day they were born, the advantage of having had children so young only comes now, when I have my whole life ahead of me and my children are no longer as needy, at least not in the same way.

"I had no conception of how demanding and unrelenting mothering is. I was unprepared for what it does to a marriage and how it takes over your life. I feel that with the first two children, it was so consuming that I lost myself. I was friendly with other women who also had children to run around all day when they were little and then after school when they got older. That was what we had in common. One day I took my third child to a playgroup for three-year-olds. Half of the mothers were working mothers and were represented by babysitters. The others were full-time mothers. I knew I didn't want to be sitting around with other mothers watching our children play for much longer. I was tapped out–I'd been at it a long time. This playgroup was at the home of a working mother, and she happened to arrive back from a business trip while we were there. Her son was thrilled to see her and she was thrilled to see him. She looked at us sitting there with envy and I looked at her with envy. At that moment, I knew there was no way to win, either you had a career and you missed your child growing up or you had no life except for your children. I wanted to change my life, but I was stuck in it."

There is an obvious division between working mothers and stay-at-home moms. The supposed compromise is represented by the part-time working mother who is accessible to her children and able to adapt her work to her children's schedule. Yet if these women are ambitious, their opportunity to get ahead is stymied by their "part-time" dedication to their job or career, if it is indeed that. For their children, however, it is as close to an ideal situation as can be.

Through the 1990s, the media reported on trends in motherhood. They included: an infertility epidemic due to women's proliferating careers (the "baby bust"), followed by a "baby boomlet" where women once again favored motherhood. The analysis is invariably cast in terms of a false distinction between stay-at-home moms and working women. In reality, most mothers today negotiate some balance between work and mothering, either simultaneously, or in successive stages of their own life and the lives of their children.

Madeleine, who is 31, has three children under the age of four, and is a full-time mother. "Later on, when my three children are grown," Madeleine says smiling, "I'll go back to work. But it doesn't seem as important as this job, of raising the children. My husband and I have discussed it and the decision is mutual. What I would like to do, however, is some kind of freelance work, perhaps in a year or two, where I can work out of the house and my oldest daughter will be in kindergarten by then. I do see these mothers going off to their offices after they drop their children at nursery school and I know it would not work for me. I feel overwhelmed and as if I am always canceling a plan with another mother, because one of the children is sick, but this is my life.

"When my husband comes home, I am too tired to do anything. He is ready to have a nice meal and relax and I have three children to get to bed. That is my night's activity. I haven't read a book or seen a new film in a long time, but I tell myself that this stage will pass. The children are adorable and I can't imagine life without them. I also know I couldn't be in two places at once. I watched my mother with her work and I know she was always stressed out. I am stressed out and I have no work, just the children. Those friends who work, even part time, look at me as if I'm spoiled, especially when I hire a sitter. Those friends who don't work know how hectic and time-consuming it is with children. More of my friends are with the children, like we wanted our mothers to be. But there is no time left for yourself. I'm just realizing this now. I really thought that if I didn't work, I'd be able to manage it. My aunts and mother all worked too, so I thought I'd be in a better position. But it's so easy to be overwhelmed, even if you have no other demands or distractions."

In sharp contrast to Madeleine's experience as a mother is Chelsea's. Having devoted her twenties and thirties to her career, Chelsea had to confront a change of status at the workplace as well as in her personal life once she had a child.

"What I had to face once my daughter was born was that I would give up certain career opportunities for her sake. I couldn't travel as much and this limited the assignments I was given. Because I was 40 when I had a child, I didn't feel denied. I realized that I was sacrificing my career path in some ways, but I knew it was a now-or-never chance to have a baby. I had to move laterally but the money was still there. It was my choice but I knew it was going to be hard for me. I did not want to give up my career for the sake of a family. Nor did I want to miss having a baby.

"I saw friends who sacrificed their entire lives to their career. These women were so consumed that they had no husband or children. I knew what my priorities were. This compromise was a big decision but not a struggle because my motivation was to raise my daughter correctly. I think that by the time I approached 40, I had attained enough in my career to accept the limitations. I was secure enough to say to the company that I had an obligation to my child and to my role as a mother. But nothing prepares you for the exhaustion of having two jobs, one as mother and the other in a career."

In 1989, Felice Schwartz suggested in her article "Management Women and the New Facts of Life" that professions and businesses have positions which are less demanding of women, if they choose them. To this end, there would be "career and family women" who would follow this track, and "career-primary women" who would remain on the fast track. The result would be that "career and family women" would not be CEOs of companies but would sustain low-pressure jobs that afforded them family time. This concept, although considerate of women's predicament, concedes that it is virtually impossible to have both—successful mothering and a stunning career. Ultimately some compromise is inevitable.

We get older without trying. The challenge is to mature at every stage. For the reasons indicated, midlife represents unique challenges but also unique opportunities, as every transitional stage in life does. When her children are grown, a woman has the chance to pursue life in directions previously denied her because of her maternal responsibilities. During adolescence both children and their parents are going through crucial developmental periods. This can be very trying, when both generations are in various forms of psychic turmoil. The parent may feel less needed, by her child as well as by her husband. Women have more options today for filling this void. They may return to school, get a job, adopt another child, or choose to have another. As we saw in the previous chapter, this transitional period also represents a crisis period in many marriages, when women look to make a new start romantically.

Then there is the phenomenon of grown children returning to the nest in early adulthood because of financial need. Although society frowns on this to a degree, it can be a welcome development for a mother who has missed the proximity of children in terms of love and companionship. Just as love in later life can be companionate rather than romantic, so relationships between mother and child can be based more on a friendship model. When a grown child moves back in the emotional boundaries will have shifted. Parents have to respect that and not revert reflexively to old, authoritarian patterns. Flexibility and communication in a non-judgmental manner are called for.

MOTHERHOOD AND WORK

- **71% of working women are mothers with children under 18**
- **The fast track is often too demanding for working mothers**
- **Many women feel conflicted about work and family**
- **Less stress in the workplace might be the answer**

Becoming a mother alters our lives forever and in many cases leaves us empty when the children are grown. For the all-consuming years in which we have little time to think for ourselves, but move like capable automatons from one stage of responsibility to the next, there is little that can satisfy us.

Even if we are acutely aware of the dilemma of how to raise our children, of what to sacrifice for their sakes–be it our own aspirations or merely the best years of our lives–in the final analysis, there is no easy solution.

Motherhood becomes a lifestyle which women inhabit, whether they are ready for it or not. Great time and energy are required to raise children. If the father is not an involved parent, Dr. Michele Kasson tells us, the role of mothering can breed resentment. "In my practice I see many women who feel overwhelmed by the expectations of mothering, especially if they work outside of the home. At the end of the day there is dinner to cook, homework to check, and chores to do. Often the working woman feels that she is not receiving enough emotional support from their husbands. Today women seek partners who are more willing to participate in the parenting and share the mundane aspects of family life."

Research conducted by McBride and Rane in 1998 suggests how important it is for wives/mothers to be confident of their husbands' skills in parenting. When a wife expresses her satisfaction with her husband as a father, he is more apt to be a part of their children's daily lives. It is evident that mothers are the nurturers, a role they have filled for centuries. In the Gable, Belsky, and Crnic study of "parental alliance," co-parenting techniques were examined. When parents undermine one another in their approach to their children, it is detrimental to the children. Ultimately it has to damage the marriage as well if the parents are not in agreement on how to handle them.

"I never agreed with anything my ex-husband did in terms of the children," says Stephanie, who at 36 is a single mother of two. "I believe that you can't really know who your husband is until you have children together. Then you see how different your value system is and how dissimilar your upbringing was. I know that when Tony and I were married, he was absent half the time. On weekends, he would play sports or watch them on television while I took care of the kids. I took the kids everywhere with me and I worked out of the house as a freelance designer until they were in grade school. I was the one who was there for them.

"It was almost as if I dreaded the weekends because the kids and I had our own rhythm during the week. Tony traveled a lot and that was almost a relief to me after a while. At first, when our son was born, I missed him when he was out of town. By the time we had a second child, I just wanted to get through. Eventually I couldn't stand how he acted with the kids and what he thought was important. And as the children grew up, I had so much trouble with his way of doing things.

"Tony never pitched in, he never did a normal thing with them, like take them to school or to the dentist. Instead he would advise them, and his style was so unlike mine that they were left confused. I guess I never knew who he really was, even before we had children, but it didn't matter then. Once I was a mother, I looked at things in a new light–I sort of came to life because I had to. The fact that Tony criticized me and told the children the opposite of what I told them was too much. That is why I wanted a divorce. To this day I wonder if we might have stayed married had we not had kids together. He never made me feel like a good mother while to the rest of the world I was doing the right thing."

Author Jessica Benjamin in her book, *The Bonds of Love*, discusses how unrealistic the expectations are for mothers. So while motherhood may be revered by society at large, mothers themselves are befuddled and may feel diminished by the role. The all-giving woman who finds fulfillment in her home and children is no longer well respected. Yet she is still considered the best possible, indeed the only complete, mother—she is still a reproach to the many who work. The moral authority of motherhood has been damaged, yet motherhood remains the backbone of care and socialization.

REVILED AND REVERED

- **The mixed message of society toward women and mothers has existed throughout history**
- **The past thirty years has raised our consciousness without offering any real solutions**
- **Motherhood is both respected and denigrated, even by our children**

We have come a long way since the trajectory of a woman's life was that of young girl, wife, mother, and grandmother. In this cycle, the motherhood phase has always been held up to us as the most meaningful. The implicit message was that the earlier years and mating period were simply a build-up to the great event of motherhood. Afterward, women were fated to slowly descend into older womanhood, an infertile time in which one's value as a grandmother gradually took precedence. Today women come to life after their children are grown, in many cases, and while they acknowledge the importance of the years spent on their children, they do not lament the passage of time and their children's adulthood.

Today, this stage in a woman's life does not necessarily define her. A woman is not only a mother, or childless, but a person who has specific interests and a certain style all her own. What is interesting to note is how many women feel that they've lost their sexuality in the process of motherhood, and will grow old without getting it back. Or, in a new spin, women in midlife, 40 to 50, do awaken sexually and emotionally as their children grow older. We look at women who exude sexuality and confidence at any age, such as the actresses Sophia Loren, Elizabeth Taylor, Goldie Hawn, and Jessica Lange. Madonna, an icon in her own right who exudes sexuality, has two children, a four-year-old daughter, Lourdes, and an infant son, Rocco. Cheryl Tiegs, a supermodel of the sixties and seventies, graced the cover of the November/December 2000 issue of MORE Magazine, talking about her new marriage to a younger man, Rod Stryker, and their twins, born to a surrogate mother. Tiegs, defying the stereotype of motherhood at the age of 53, is quoted as saying, "It's better than being a grandmother!" Each of these women has set an example as mothers who have also followed their own path throughout their childbearing years and have not missed a beat in either arena.

Despite the glamour and determination of these celebrity moms, the stereotypical image of mothers is difficult to dispel. As Shere Hite remarks in *The Hite Report on the Family*, "In the patriarchal mind, the mother is thought of as asexual, mothers being 'good,' the opposite of 'loose women.' Mothers are thought of as older women whilst their daughters are 'Lolitas' and 'sexpots'." And so, in the cycle of life, we are encouraged to give over our sexuality, our youth and our beauty to our daughters, who will meet with the same fate as their mothers in turn.

Emma, at 44, has been a mother for eighteen years. Recently she has come to terms with the fact that she will not be having any more children.

"I have been absorbed in the role of mothering my two children for so long that I both count the days until my twelve-year-old leaves the house and also dread when the time comes. I thought I was prepared for mothering when I was 26, but in retrospect, how could I have been? It was great to have a baby, the ultimate plaything, but as these children grew, I realized that mothering takes you by surprise. It is one thing after another and it is not within our control.

"I was close with my own mother growing up but she never emphasized that I should marry and have kids. I gave up a fast-track job for my children, and I moved across the country for my husband. Yet I don't feel there was anything about this life that caused me to miss out. I know I gave up some of myself for my kids and that after I had a second child, it was obvious that I would not be on a career path anymore. But I also knew that I could put my energy elsewhere, like into the PTA and into volunteer work at a soup kitchen. This is how I organized my life. The difference for me from other women my age is that I was in touch with my feelings, I knew what I had done."

In a manner similar to Emma, Jackie has found motherhood to be containable. At the age of 39, she is the mother to one eleven-year-old daughter. "I have been married for thirteen years and it has been an even keel all the way. I knew what to expect from my husband because we dated for so many years. What prepared me for motherhood was having a sister who was ten years younger. Our mother was a full-time working mother and I basically raised this sister. She was like my child and caring for her made me aware of my maternal instincts. I doubt that I would have known what to do if not for her.

"Although my mother worked, which was sort of unusual for her day, it was not so much her influence as that of my co-workers that influenced my view of mothering and careers. When I was single and working, I saw how much the women in the office struggled once they had babies and planned to keep their jobs. Maybe my mother handled it better, or I saw it from a different perspective when I was younger, but the women who were my age or even ten years older who had kids were so stressed out. This made me think I would not work when I had a small child. In the end I have had a career all along, without missing a beat because of finances, and because I love what I do.

"What I have learned as the years go by is that my work actually balances my mothering and keeps it calmer. I only have one child, and my perspective would be so skewed if not for work. The negative with one child is that a mother tends to dote on that child, and for my daughter's sake my preoccupation with work is the saving grace. I know that I could have become one of those mothers who is completely absorbed by her kid. It's almost like work has shown me how to be a calmer mother. And as my daughter grows up, I feel I'm equipped for any direction that life takes me."

DISCOVERY AND RESOLUTION

- **Once we become mothers, our lives change**
- **Caring for our children is an all-consuming occupation**
- **Society expects it of us**
- **Women feel incomplete without it**

On the other hand there are women who are compelled to mother in a specific way, and are swayed by external values. The U.S. Department of Labor reports that 71 percent of working women have children under eighteen years of age. The impetus to work is not always about personal fulfillment, but about putting food on the table, and in many cases purchasing a certain brand of clothing for her children, or a coveted toy. In recent years the motivation to make money has been driven by the media, and this extends to the realm of parenting where influence and a herd mentality is found in many circles. On October 12th, 2000, a full-page advertisement campaign for Mercedes-Benz Manhattan was inaugurated, with a tag line which read, "If their Daddies could buy them CLKs, so could yours." The bottom of the ad read, "At Mercedes-Benz Manhattan, your Daddy will be surprised at how affordable a new or pre-owned CLK can be, and how easy it would be for him to prove that you're still your Daddy's little girl." According to Nancy Hass' article in *The New York Times* on October 22, 2000, this advertisement evoked an outcry from mothers who did not appreciate the message being sent to their adolescent daughters. Nor did fathers approve the idea that they could buy their daughters with extravagant presents. Mercedes-Benz obviously had not anticipated a negative reaction. Their target audience was a parent body that pampers their children. The program includes the right schools, the right friends, and the right material possessions, to launch these children into the world with every advantage.

Such superficiality may be the legacy of the generation of babyboomer mothers. The myriad of women who married early and may or may not have had multiple marriages, have "band-aided" themselves in a less than adequate marriage with material goods, instead of being introspective. In return, the husbands have worked hard to sustain their wives' habits. As mothers, these women have passed this feeding frenzy of objects on to their children, who are already in the midst of a media/glam culture. If the wives/mothers pacify themselves with a satisfying lifestyle, their children tend to emulate it. So when the mother becomes disillusioned, and breaks free, the "ideal" environment may be taken away from her children, the better for her to find herself. The selfish/selfless mother becomes unglued.

FINDING ONESELF
AT THE CHILDREN'S EXPENSE

A less than happy marriage can be appeased by a material world. When the mother/wife decides to leave, risking lifestyle for her true self, her children are left in the lurch. Motherhood has always been about selflessness. Nothing else is acceptable.

"There is no question that my children have been spoiled," admits Kathy, who at 40 decided she had to be divorced. "I know that one family lives better than two parts of a divided family. I struggled for years with this decision and I was very spoiled. It wasn't only about my children, but about how I would survive without having the luxuries I was accustomed to. After twelve years, I really couldn't be married to my husband, and I asked for a divorce. My main concern was the children, and I felt sick inside over breaking up the family. It never occurred to me that they would resent the lack of riches that were a result of the divorce. I had been the one who spoiled them and I was the perpetrator when it all fell apart.

"In the Catholic religion, children are everything and breaking up the family is considered a sin. I wrestled with this for so long, I thought about my children and how much I loved them. I would give my life for my four children and yet I couldn't be married to their father another minute. After having focused on them for ten years, without any other part of my life having as much weight, I simply had to get me back. To this day, I think that I was brainwashed into believing mothering was the living end. And when you mix that kind of responsibility with a bounty of riches, everything loses its center."

If mothers send out mixed messages to their children when it comes to consumerism, it isn't completely their fault. As we know, mothers are caregivers, nurturers, and ultimately peacemakers and pleasers. If it pleases our children, we are apt to go along. This has been our role from time immemorial. Today, mothering is entangled with materialism in a new way. While the 1980s were dubbed the era of opulence and glamour, the return to this mind-set is exponential, and the results far exceed those of twenty years ago. Journalist Amy Finnerty wrote an editorial on October 20, 2000 in the *Wall Street Journal* entitled "The Tween Menace: Young girls, 'sophisticated' tastes. Try shopping with your daughter now." Finnerty writes about the "teenification of children's fashion" and the fact that their role models are not yet adults themselves. An example of this is Britney Spears, pop singer to millions of early teens, primarily girls. What confuses the issue for mothers and their teenage daughters is what Finnerty refers to as the "infantilization of women's fashion," where women's shops cater to the bodies of young girls, and there is no distinction between women's wear for mothers and other adult women, on the one hand, and our daughters, from age ten upward, on the other. As thirteen-year-old daughters accuse their mothers of wearing clothing more appropriate for their peers, forty-year-old mothers are equally surprised at finding their taste in clothes to be identical to their daughters'. If there are no parameters when it comes to wardrobes for mothers and their adolescent daughters, one can only wonder about the traditional role of mothering, and the position of respect that has always been a mother's entitlement.

MIXED MESSAGES
FOR MOTHERS AND DAUGHTERS

- **Mothers and daughters find themselves shopping for the same wardrobe and accessories**

- **Daughters believe their mothers are encroaching on their style**

- **Mothers feel their daughters are trespassing on their territory**

- **The breakdown of hierarchy spreads to other areas of the mother–child relationship**

"I have given up on shopping with my daughters," sighs Alena, who at 45 has been married for 17 years. "Either I have to change my style or shop in a more conservative way, or we have to share clothes. I no longer see clothes for women that teenage and college girls don't think are made for them. My daughters and I fight when we shop and I feel like an inadequate mother if I don't buy them what they want, which is often something I would buy for myself. The whole ordeal makes me feel uneasy and my memories of shopping with my mother are so pleasant, while the reality with my daughters is not.

"In a strange way, this becomes an issue between me and my girls. It sounds ridiculous, but I'm beginning to realize that one aspect of mothering that is supposed to be fun and a perk is now weighed down by some media message that fifteen-year-old models in designer clothes give to our kids."

So often we have heard that young children are a delight, albeit physically exhausting. The unconditional love and pure dependency of young children seems to evaporate as our children hit adolescence. And while this has always been the case, it is exacerbated today by the speed with which our children outgrow their childhood. For many mothers, there is a sense of loss long before their children approach college age and leave home.

At 40, which is a turning point for women, we are better able to let go, and be more accepting of what mothering is about today. The endless care and relentless time and energy put into our children have not become passé, but the nature of the relationship between mother and child has changed. Once again, the fast-paced life we lead today has an impact on how soon this happens in our children's lives and our response to it. "Women, even mothers, are looking for serenity and peace by 40," Antoinette Michaels, relationship expert, explains. "Now they choose how to spend their time. If their children are one piece of their lives that has not gone perfectly or has been filled with surprises, then this is when some letting go has to happen. It is almost as if these women have been asleep since they were teenagers and the obstacle to their own self-fulfillment had much to do with husbands and children."

LETTING GO

Mothering is not an unmitigated bliss, no matter what society implies. Young mothers may not realize this for many years. For those women who become mothers in their late thirties or early forties, there is greater awareness of the pros and cons of motherhood.

"I became a single mother when I filed for divorce three years ago," Janet, at 46, tells us. "My kids were totally aware of what had gone on and why I wanted a divorce. They seemed very supportive at first, especially my daughters. And communication is key: I have been honest with the kids from the beginning. And at first that seemed to be the right way to go. The kids were very empathetic. I don't believe in blowing sunshine or pretending anything. I am very proud of my children, and one daughter encouraged me to leave because she didn't want me to suffer anymore.

"At the same time, I misconstrued the fallout of divorce because later my children took their father's side. Maybe they don't consider me a good mother on some level for wanting a divorce. I feel like I'm just spreading my wings after years of mothering and being blind in a marriage. Being a single mother is another story altogether. No one prepared me for that. Women aren't even treated the same way if they are single mothers, at least in a small town or suburb. So while my life is improving, my children see me as less of a mother. Maybe I should have divorced years ago, when they were small, and the adjustment would not have been so great. I stayed for them so they could have an intact family and a 'perfect' mother."

According to the U.S. Census Bureau, in 1997 60 percent of births to single women were to white mothers. Seventy percent of African-American births, 41 percent of Hispanic, and 22 percent of non-Hispanic white births occurred outside marriage. The stigma attached to single motherhood—whether unwed, divorced, widowed or never married by choice—is decreasing. And like divorce, the sheer force of numbers is what reconciles the status of single mothers to our culture. The past twenty years have seen great changes in these "categories" of motherhood. While fifty years ago, the shame associated with unwed motherhood or single parenting was acute, today there is the recognition that this role is here to stay, with tacit acceptance at worst.

Single mothers, however, find there is a definite bias against them. The SAA of the 21st Century (formerly the Stepfamily Association of America) reports that 23 percent of children under 18 live only with their biological mother. And 26 percent of children under 18 live in some stepfamily arrangement. The parenting responsibilities in a stepfamily are not evenly distributed; often the parent in the new marriage parents alone, while the stepparent remains remote. Therefore single mothers, although they may be in a new marriage, continue to be single mothers to their children. There are nearly 10 million single household families in the U.S. today, according to the 2000 Census, three-quarters of which are run by women/ mothers. Demographers now predict that more than half of children born in the 1990s will spend at least part of their childhood in a single-parent home.

SINGLE MOTHERHOOD

- **23% of children under 18 live with single biological mothers**
- **26% of children under 18 live in some sort of stepfamily**
- **Approval for single mothers is slow but steady**

Birthrates are highest among women between the ages of 20 and 24 but the rate for older single mothers has increased 128 percent for white women in their thirties between 1970 and 1994. More women can now afford to be single mothers, and they have many options: sperm banks, adoption, getting pregnant by an acquaintance whom they don't intend to be involved with as a partner–in addition to the traditional chance pregnancy by a lover. Even under the best of conditions, single motherhood is a long, hard journey for both mother and children. Children living outside marriage are seven times more likely to experience poverty and seventeen times more likely to end up on welfare and to have a propensity for emotional problems, discipline problems, and early pregnancy. But the results are not uniformly negative; it is a matter of relative probability. Experts believe the majority of these children will do just fine.

"I felt very responsible for my daughter," begins Joy, who at

50 has been a single working mother for the past twelve years. "I knew that I could do it and that my job afforded me the opportunity. But I made all of the choices by myself for Amanda, my daughter, and there were advantages and disadvantages. I know that at school she had some explaining to do, but on the other hand, it also gave her a kind of inner strength. There were very few children with the same situation in our town and this forced Amanda to believe in herself.

"I am very proud of the outcome, but there have been moments. I decided when she was born that I wanted us to be religious on some level. I wanted her to be confirmed and I wanted religion to be a part of her upbringing. Since I'd never had much religion, I had to start from scratch too. After her confirmation, I think she was slightly skeptical. But this is also the age; adolescent girls can behave this way. What mattered to me was that I could pay for schooling and that money would not be an issue. Children are very expensive, and I knew that I would be responsible in every way because there was no one to share that responsibility with. And in times of trouble, there was no one to share the burden. Although I was prepared for this by virtue of having a baby without a spouse, in my late thirties, I never quite anticipated how much I was on my own until the years went by. In some ways it is more trying as a kid gets older."

No matter when a woman has a child, the experience alters her life irreversibly. While women believe that they can have freedom and still mother or not, the reality is that motherhood is very demanding, and our thought processes change. Even the most selfish of women become selfless as mothers. Those of us who have postponed motherhood in order to achieve for ourselves, discover that once the child is born, we are situated in a similar place emotionally. The big difference has to do with finances, mind set, life experience, and maturity. There are those women who choose to marry, and consequently mother, later. Others miss the opportunity to marry and perhaps to mother while focusing on other parts of their lives.

MIND-SET AND EXPERIENCE

Women today, more than ever before, are conscious of what is required to be a mother. Some opt to postpone mothering in order to live a full life first, others end up mothering late by virtue of life choices, i.e., careers and late marriage.

Amber, who has been married for twenty-six years, is the mother of three boys, aged thirteen, ten, and seven. Having married at 21, Amber regards her determination to have children after twelve years of marriage as a wise decision.

"I was so sheltered growing up that marriage was a rude shock for me. When I saw my sister struggle with her kids, it only made me want children less. I was also very career-oriented and my husband understood that. The first five years of the marriage he did not want children either, and then he changed. Ten years into the marriage I was getting pressure from him, from family members, from everyone. I kept hitting a fork in the road in my career, and there was always the implicit expectation that I would have babies eventually. I might not have understood what life would be like without the experience of mothering, but I also understood what it would be like to take care of a colicky baby, and the amount of work that went into it. I kept watching my sister and she kept having kids and I kept wanting to run away from it.

"By the time I had my boys, I was ready for another chapter of my marriage. And even with that attitude, I had no idea it would be so overwhelming. When the boys were small, I was too busy with them to see that the marriage was affected to the degree it was. Now I look back and I see that mothering took over my life–that I changed. I stopped thinking about myself and started thinking about the boys. I knew from the start how much of a responsibility it was. I knew this because I was older. The really young mothers don't know it, but if you wait, it's because you do know it. I was as prepared as one can be–but you are never prepared. My mother says there are two jobs no one is ever prepared for, being a mother and being President of the United States. I know what she means. But I see myself as someone who could have had a few different careers, and I took the one that would least affect my children. I am thrilled to be a mother, and later in life I am wiser, and more affluent. Who knew I would be so exhausted? I do not regret my decision, but it dawns on me, even now, years into it, that this is an unending commitment. The emotional rewards for me, as someone who might have skipped having kids, exceed my expectations."

Of the women interviewed on mothering, the babyboomers, as so often is the case, seem to be the ones most invested in the fantasy of motherhood and happy-ever-after. As Antoinette Michaels, relationship expert, remarks, no matter what generation we are from, we get mixed messages about what motherhood should mean. "There are different kinds of mothers," explains Michaels, "and there are specific styles of mothering. It is important for a mother to know why she does what she does and what motivates her to raise her children as she does." There are those women who are "Peter Pan mothers," and would like to remain young mothers forever. Other mothers treat their children like puppies and resist the inevitable aging process, preferring them as little children. Many are martyrs who sacrifice themselves for their children, and who live vicariously through their children's achievements. Today's parents are unique compared to previous generations in that they are having fewer children, and they aspire to be perfect parents for those children. Families today are more child-centered than ever before; many parents are totally invested in their children's happiness and success.

TYPES OF MOTHERS

- **Peter Pan mothers: Those who wish to remain young forever**

- **Children as puppies: Those mothers wish their children would never grow up**

- **Martyrs: Those who sacrifice themselves for their children**

- **Older/grandmother mothers: Those who have children late in life**

- **Vicarious mothers: who live through their children's achievements**

- **Healthy mothers: Those who are wide awake in their role and accepting of the limitations and the joys of mothering**

There is no perfect time to have a baby, and beginning a family revolutionizes one's life; there is no going back to a time before the children existed. Mothering, more than any other experience in life for women, challenges us emotionally, physically, and mentally. Most notable is how many women felt unprepared for some aspect of motherhood, regardless of when they became mothers and under what conditions. In time, and with experience, mothers stop pretending that mothering is an idyllic state, but accept that it is one with challenges and rich rewards. The more self-aware we become, the more powerful we become in mothering—as in our other roles in life.

8

Missing Links / Friends and Family

When it comes to friendships, women do not respond as men do, and, by the same token, women need friendships and connections in a way men do not. Female relationships differ from male relationships, and of course, much of our behavior as friends has been conditioned by our mother's patterns with her own friends. This, again, is an underlying theme, that our mothers, as our first love relationship, have set the example for our ability to be close with others. This is compounded by the fact that women and men have unique needs when it comes to friendship, and rely on this relationship to different degrees.

Alice Michaeli, sociologist, tells us: "Males can spend ten years away from a friend and get together without even having to catch up. Men expect less whereas women expect so much. On the other hand, if a woman breaks off a friendship, it is because it doesn't fit in with her family, or suit her marriage." Here then is another example of a woman being compliant and adopting compromise as a solution. If she could meet on her own time a friend whom her husband does not appreciate, rather than sever the bond, it can work for both husband and wife.

When at the age of 49 Meredith had a falling out with her best friend, she realized it had been years in the making. "It took me so long to understand that just because Kerri and I had been close in childhood didn't mean that we had to be close as adult women. Our mothers were best friends and we were expected to be the same. She came from another part of the country and during high school we talked on the phone a great deal. As we got older, I saw that Kerri had difficulty with people and was unable to attach to anyone. But she was attached to me and that made me think the friendship was important.

"Every time we fought there were these blow-ups and she took offense at what I said. It was all about her, and the 'us' of the relationship was about how it affected her. Now we were adult women and like so many women, we were both in fields where we were overworked and underpaid. I met someone, late in life, and married him. She was ambivalent about my engagement—I think she was envious. She did not appreciate my happiness, which was the last straw for me. She is single to this day and I believe that is a part of her anger toward me. I had taken enough abuse from the relationship and I no longer wanted to apologize for anything. It had actually been an abusive friendship and I couldn't face it for years. I kept expecting it to be something else, something good. I had been raised to believe it was a special friendship. I hung on for so long because I did not understand the dynamic until recently. Today it is finished."

Although some women are better equipped psychologically to manage the ups and downs of female camaraderie, it has been established that friendships in general are critical for women. Scientists believe, according to *Prevention Magazine's* December 2000 issue, that those who have more human contact can live twice as long as those who are isolated. With women at a seven-and-a-half-year advantage over men in terms of longevity, we can attribute a part of this longer, healthier life span to a woman's ability to have intimate connections with their friends. Women are willing to share their innermost feelings with their female friends. Yet there are reasons why a friendship will break up, despite a history of trading confidences; there are many chances and alterations in a woman's life that require new and ongoing friendships.

The objective materials which constitute the basis for friendship are lifestyle, common values, socioeconomic status and education. Yet these links are not the only ones. It is possible for two women of disparate backgrounds to come together and bond on a spiritual level. What contributes most often to the end of female friendships has to do with trust, loyalty and betrayal. "Two women can be friends with every commonality and if one does something to the other, the friendship is suddenly and irrevocably over," Alice Michaeli, sociologist, believes. "From a sociological point of view, this act will be considered the first and final deviant act. It is the end of a friendship. They may remain in superficial contact, but the closeness they formerly shared will never be recovered. Friendships between women often end over a rigidity or controlling element in one woman's personality, which will lead to a particularly damaging incident. Changes in lifestyle are also terminal factors."

Anna, who is 47, introduced her best friend from childhood, Ruby, to Mark. Mark and Ruby eventually married. Anna was not invited to the wedding. Why? Anna had an adoptive daughter, who was full of youthful high spirits and could be unruly. Ruby was a control freak, and was determined that everything at the wedding go smoothly, and that all the attention be on them. She tried to explain that neglecting to invite Anna to the wedding was an oversight, or a misunderstanding about schedule. But Anna knew her friend very well, and realized that her controlling nature lay behind the decision. She never confronted Ruby about it, but today their friendship is perfunctory and they only see each other at parties a couple of times a year. Irreversible breaks of this sort between friends are more common among women than men—even though women also prize friendship much more highly.

Female friendships begin early and cause great joy or devastation as they play out. Author Shere Hite in *The Hite Report on the Family* indicates that only 10 percent of the girls she interviewed did not have a best female friend. The 90-percent majority of teenage girls viewed their best friend as someone "with whom they share their feelings, experiences and plans for the future." The fact that adolescent boys feel social pressure to disassociate from girls makes female friendships all the more meaningful. This female requirement carries over into adulthood, and even after marriage and motherhood, women seem to be in constant search of close, understanding female friends.

"I have learned the hard way with friendship," explains Marguerite, who at 36 is enrolled in college part time and works part time. "My family did not have money but we were raised to be close and to devote ourselves to each other. I had a friend who was from my hometown and our mothers were very close. It felt like we were relatives more than friends. And because our mothers were close, I thought I could trust this friend. My whole upbringing had been about family, then friends, and I believed she and I were close. So when I moved to California when I turned 30 and finally escaped, I invited her to visit. She was very snobby and put on airs but I tried to ignore it because my mother was so pleased that she was visiting. In fact she visited several times, for long stays, once for over three months. I paid for almost everything during her visits, and she never paid me back although she and I understood my putting out the money to be a loan. Then, after she got to know her way around and met a man, she stopped leaning on me altogether and we were no longer in touch. That is what shocked me most of all.

"What bothers me so much about this is that we are both from the same culture. We are Hispanic women who come from very sheltered families where leaving home and going to school has not been done before. I chose to leave and to go

199

across the country to learn what it is like to be on my own and to have a career. I wanted to know what was out there beyond our small lives. I thought that this friend shared the same vision. I wanted to break free and I thought we could do some of that together. The twist is that she was part of what forced me to get over my naivete. Instead of this friend being a buffer in a foreign world, she became a major roadblock. Thanks to her I have learned not to be so trusting and I have learned that just because my mother is family-oriented and counts on her friends, doesn't mean that I have something in common with her friends or extended family members."

There are several elements to Marguerite's story. If there is a competition between female friends, on any level, it gets in the way of a healthy, honest relationship. And forced friendships, such as the one she described, or friendships of convenience, cannot meet the test of time. Most striking of all, however, is the issue of finding a man and forgetting your girlfriend. This is an age-old occurrence, with mixed messages coming from our mothers and teachers since grade school. Since girls are raised to be in search of the ideal mate as savior, a female friendship often suffers during the trials and tribulations of her best friend's love life. It may take years of friendship contemporaneous with a love life for a woman to understand that romance does not have to be the priority. We have been conditioned to think that a man comes first, and if others suffer, be it family members or friends, so be it. Since we do it to each other, women rally to their friend's defense when a love relationship is in decline.

FRIENDSHIP AFTER ROMANCE

We have been trained to put our friends second to our lovers. Once the lover fails us, we run back to our friends.

"The women I know who are evolved do not isolate themselves once they find a partner," Antoinette Michaels, relationship expert, claims. "It might take years for a woman to break this pattern where she will distance herself from her best friends while she is falling in love with a new man. The friendships are not a priority as long as things are going well. As soon as the relationship goes badly, that woman is back on the phone to her friends, confiding every problem in the relationship." This unfaithfulness to one's gender occurs early in a girl's life. Her friendship is put aside when a boyfriend enters the picture and the girl believes she is expected to choose between her best friend and her boyfriend.

By the age of 40, a woman might recognize the folly of this pattern of putting the man ahead of the friendship and attempt a better balance. Another factor with friendships is that they change as our lives are altered. Women in particular seem to have friendships that are affected by circumstances. When a woman's status changes and she becomes divorced or married, or has a child, she and her closest friends may no longer be in the same place in their lives. A part of the distance that occurs may be a matter of perception, i.e. a woman feels she is not wanted by her married friends once she is divorced. Or a woman who is a stay-at-home mother might not feel she is any longer the equal of her friend who has climbed the corporate ladder.

Geography is another piece of the friendship equation. In our mobile society, we make friends wherever we go as a matter of convenience. While women do miss old friends, the need for new friendship is ever-present. Often women seek female friendships because a husband or partner may not emote. A woman will look for an emotional response to her issues and finds that her female friends will listen.

Of course, there is always the possibility that a man will come between best friends. This threat does not go away in later age; the high incidence of divorce ensures that the scenario can recur in middle age.

"Two years ago, when my four children were under the age of seven, we moved out to a town from a city," Gwenievere begins. "This was because my husband was relocated. I was very isolated and in the car constantly. I missed my friends who were far away and there was very little that could console me. I joined a reading club in order to meet other women. There was a woman named May who became my close friend and confidante. We would meet for coffee and we had our sons in the same class in school. Eventually we went out for dinner as couples. I noticed that she spoke mostly with my husband and that she was slightly flirtatious. She always admired any gift he gave me and she seemed to watch us closely, how we lived and when we went on vacations. Her life was similar but she seemed to want more things, more possessions.

"When I told May that I was unhappily married, she told

me that she was too. We both ended up getting divorced at the same time. I moved to the next town and rented an apartment. She even helped me move out of the house. Then I heard through other friends that she was dating my ex-husband. I couldn't believe it because we were spending so much time together. I couldn't believe that I was so blind that I didn't see this happening. One night she brought her son over to my apartment because she was meeting my ex-husband. We had a confrontation and she basically said if I didn't want him, he was up for grabs. I have never spoken to her since. The relationship she had with my ex-husband lasted about six months. During that period, my children were with her a great deal of the time. My youngest son kept asking me why I wasn't with May anymore when they went out for pancakes."

Trust, of course, is one of the most meaningful elements in a friendship, and implicit in this trust is the expectation that there will be no betrayal. A story such as Gwenievere's, which in outline, unfortunately, is not uncommon, raises serious questions about the integrity of the female bond when men come into the picture. Margaret Atwood has explored this theme in a couple of her novels, including *Cat's Eye* and *The Robber Bride*. In the latter book, Antonia, Karen, and Roz are three 50-ish Toronto friends, pals since college, all of whom have had to negotiate (none too well) the treacheries of another friend, Zenia—someone who in the past has stolen a significant man from each of the others. *Cat's Eye* involves a friendship beginning in adolescence between Elaine, the narrator of the tale, and Cordelia, her best friend and intermittent torturer. For all that transpires between the two friends as young girls and young women, it is only when Elaine, as a woman in midlife, faces the demons of the friendship and awakens to her own needs, that the toxic nature of the relationship is finally understood. Women invest a great deal in their relationships with other women, but as women awaken to themselves in adulthood, these friendships sometimes don't survive the personal growth—the awakening—of either one of the friends. Female friendships are deeper than those between men, yet, at the same time, more fragile.

TRUST AND BETRAYAL

Female friendships end when a trust is broken or one friend has betrayed the other. The friendship suffers irreparable damage. If there is regret and the two friends recognize the loss, it will still not be remedied.

There are episodes in one's life outside the triangle of a friend, her ex-husband/ex-lover, and her best friend, that also bring home the reality of having less than satisfying or dependable friends. In Carolanne's situation, her widowhood alerted her to the meaning of friendship.

"Being all alone teaches you how not to be afraid," says Carolanne who, at age 43, was widowed unexpectedly four years ago. "Now people treat me differently, with pity, especially people I have met recently. The truth is, I lost a whole life and even my close friends and family are not the same. I was no longer welcome in certain groups and people who I thought were my friends and a connection, stopped being that for me. It wasn't my choice and I am not the one who chose to bail out; I think that happens in some cases. But once my husband died, people did it to me. You learn who your true friends are in a heartbeat after a tragedy. There were women, friends and even cousins, who I thought I could count on, who saw me as a threat once I was single. I thought they would be helping me and instead they were staying away from me. I never anticipated losing so much so fast."

Because we tend to repeat our own family history, as Katherine Rabinowitz, psychotherapist, has explained earlier, we end up making poor choices in friendships, as in other parts of our lives. "There are women who can't find lasting friendships and always end up feeling betrayed. All of this is because of the influence of their family history which continues to exert an unconscious force on their choices, creating repeated patterns, that only get broken after the underlying dynamics are exposed and worked through over time."

It is uplifting to hear of friendships that have survived a crisis or have been resurrected as a result of a kind of personal revelation, or even those that have survived life's stresses and changes. A recent article published in the November 2000 issue of OPRAH Magazine by Mark Matousek entitled "Friends For Life?" focuses on the complexities of lasting female friendship. "There are no formulas, no rule books for maneuvering through the minefield of this delicate relationship," Matousek writes, as he explores the bond from the point of view of eight women writers. Amy Bloom, author of *A Blind*

Man Can See How Much I Love You, describes her friend's battle with breast cancer. "I realized once again that what and who we are in everyday life is sharpened and focused in crisis!" says Bloom. The illness brought the two friends together in a profound way. "We now know how much our lives have to offer us and how stupid and ungrateful we would be if we did not take advantage of those gifts."

SURVIVAL IN FRIENDSHIP

- **Once female friends survive a crisis, they become closer**
- **They can count on each other and act as a shield against the world**

"My family lives so far away and has for the past sixteen years," Samantha tells us, "that my girlfriends are my family. I have hung on so tightly to these friends and it has been worth everything. Frank, my husband, is not always very kind and I know he has been jealous of my time spent with my close circle of friends. There is one friend who he really doesn't like because I am on the phone with her so much. I will tell her everything and he knows it. I would not tell him much at all. So maybe she replaces him or maybe it's a need that he can't fill and so I seek her out. I also hold onto these friendships because my in-laws are not good to me and I don't have much respect for them.

"I was very young when I got married and I didn't know that Frank's parents wouldn't be on my side and would actually find fault with me. I didn't know how much I would miss my parents and my brother and sister who live three thousand miles away. Then it was my reality and I was miserable. Until I had established these friendships, I was adrift. Then I looked to these new friendships that were built on what we each lacked in our marriages and families. My two best friends also have parents who live far away. We talk about how awful it is all the time. And these friends help me to see how wrong things can be in our lives and also to face them and to be strong. I find them to be a buffer for me. I know now that I need these friends more than ever before. My children are getting older and my husband is not easy. The friendships help me through the rough parts. I couldn't survive without them."

COURAGEOUS ACTS

It requires courage to discard negative friendships. The decision is liberating and puts us on a better course.

Best friends are not always appreciated because women lack the requisite self-esteem. If we look to our husbands to be our best friends, ultimately we may be disappointed. While a husband fills other needs such as provider, father to our children, and lover, he cannot by definition be a best friend. While there are other qualities in a marriage that mirror those of a best friendship, and some attributes are shared, the responsibility is fundamentally different. Female friendships, on the other hand, require patience, acceptance, and nurturance to survive. In a woman's psychic awakening, certain friendships will need to be reevaluated, revised—and maybe left behind.

A woman's relationships with other female family members has a different dynamic. "I now know that how my mother raised me has everything to do with how I relate to my friends and in-laws," says Allison, who at 49, has been widowed for five years. "My mother is a woman who cannot give any emotion out or take any emotion in. So I never learned how to be secure in my own emotions, and that caused problems in relationships and friendships. I didn't know how to create my own space and to separate. My mother had never done this and I had no one to teach me. I didn't know how to do a time out with people, whether it was a love relationship, a familial one, or a friendship. If there was an argument and I perceived it as a matter of principle as opposed to fact in a specific incident, I let it become a big issue. I would lose touch with people, and I would not be able to recover from a fall. And there would be long stretches when I couldn't deal with my mother at all.

"What helped me the most was realizing that my feelings counted, and not trying to figure out how to behave in every instance. I was taught nothing, but my mother-in-law helped to teach me. I learned that no one is perfect and no friend or family member can save you. If I could have had my mother and my mother-in-law put in a blender into one person, that person would have been close to ideal. Instead, I paid attention to my husband's family, and to my closest friends. I saw what I had missed in my own upbringing. I took this lesson to heart and I raised my daughters with the missing links filled in. And it took many years to really see it the right way for myself."

If our mothers have exerted power over us and we go out into the world and repeat what we know, there will be rocky times with our female friends. Female friendships are an imitation of what daughters have shared with their mothers. Daughters often have a love/hate relationship with their mother. Consciously or unconsciously, this ambivalence migrates to all their female friends. In loving a best female friend, then, the woman makes her friend suffer, just as her mother made her suffer. Given this, it seems that women would be doomed to unsuccessful connections—not only to their mothers, but to their female friends as well. As women begin to mature, however, they respect and value their female friends more. While the early motivation and commonality for friendship and companionship might not withstand the test of time, these deep and loyal female connections do.

Nancy Chodorow explains in her essay "Family Structure and Feminine Personality" that personality development is "not the result of conscious parental intention." Our personality is influenced by our upbringing but is also individual and based on unique character traits. These character traits cause us to react as we do in specific situations with friends and family. It is coming to understand our individual needs in relation to the world of friends and family that is key.

The mother–daughter issue is one of such gravity it commands volumes of exploration—and sometimes a lifetime of effort to work out. For our purposes, the mother–daughter bond is viewed within the context of how women reclaim themselves. Several interviewees have discussed how profoundly their mother's influence has been when it comes to their siblings, spouses, and friends. The standard wisdom involves fathers, as well. The paradox for daughters/women is that they idealize their fathers instead of their mothers, whom they denigrate. The irony is that mothers and daughters, being the same gender, should band together. Often both generations work against each other instead, with inadequate self-worth on either side. This is a socially induced condition. These daughters then grow up with self-esteem issues because they have not respected their female role model, their mothers. A less negative point of view is that although there have been issues between mothers and daughters, as the relationship evolves and the daughter enters adulthood there can be a satisfying meeting ground. In this scenario, both mother and daughter achieve a healthy consciousness.

"When I got married, fifteen years ago," says Marte, who has been divorced for four years, "my husband and my mother did not get along. I had to choose and I chose my husband. Then we had two sons and I needed my mother because I was overwhelmed. She came to my help, but I had to see her when my husband was at work and that was when she was with the boys. I felt like there were two camps and I was allowed in both. My mother did not approve of my husband's values which on some level were becoming mine. I couldn't be with my husband and not live the lifestyle he wanted. And I liked parts of it, I really did, although my mother saw me as materialistic."

"Things were so bad between my mother and my husband that on holidays I had to decide. My husband has no extended family, no one who lives nearby, and so we were alone on those days. I hated it, and felt so lonely. It was not how I was raised and not how I wanted to raise my boys. My husband fooled me into thinking that it didn't matter if we didn't do the holidays with my family, as long as we had each other. I look back now, after my divorce, and I regret those years. I do every holiday with my mother and brother now and I feel like I am in touch with myself."

Our society reinforces a belief that a man comes first and that the marriage and family of procreation are more important than the family of origin. What is sad about Marte's experience is that she was unable to find a compromise solution and integrate the two. Instead she forfeited her own needs for her husband's. Once her marriage dissolved, however, she relied once again on her mother. This can happen in reverse as well, where a daughter sees her mother putting her new marriage first and feels threatened. When a mother and daughter have been very close and the mother, who is single, finds a partner, the daughter may feel that she now comes second to the relationship. "It is not that the relationship is more important than the mother–daughter bond," explains Dr. Michele Kasson, "but many women in their forties or fifties with grown daughters may not feel as though they have many chances left. As the daughters will be moving on to their own lives outside of the mother–daughter relationship, the mother may feel it is time to expand her options beyond her biological family."

CHOICES

If a choice has to be made between

husband and mother or daughter and new husband, women often opt for the man. This has been encouraged by our culture. If a daughter finds herself a single mother one day, she will put this relationship first as well.

Ideally, we would be able to find a balance between our families of origin and our families of procreation, and a peaceful coexistence could be established. Short of this, however, a myriad of problems emerge. For single women in midlife, the attachment to their mothers is complicated as well. Many times a mother will be looking for a specific life for her daughter long after it has become evident that this is not her daughter's desire nor will it be her reality. A mother who hopes that her daughter will emulate her life might be in for a shock. Mothers who step back and accept that their daughters have to seek their own destiny are more realistic—the world today is not the world they knew. Their experience at 35 cannot be compared to their daughters' experience at 35.

Without necessarily meaning to set an example, babyboomers have shown their daughters the value of self-sufficiency. These daughters observe their mothers divorced and job hunting today, earning degrees they originally pursued twenty-five years earlier. They recognize their mothers' lives as a mid-century fiction. These daughters will not count on a man to complete their lives in the same way that their mothers did, particularly in middle and upper-middle class marriages. If anything, the younger women will extend their schooling and their careers, thus postponing the responsibilities that their mothers had so early on: that of children and husbands. They might not rush to incorporate children and husbands into the picture, having seen it can be less than perfect.

EXAMPLES SET

Enough female babyboomers have found themselves single without a career to be a cautionary tale for their daughters. Those babyboomers whose ambition and idealism resulted in exhaustion, and depletion, are also a cautionary example for their daughters.

"My mother used to say to me, if only I could put my head on your shoulders," says Eileen, who is 42. "I look back now and I know that I should have listened. I spent years with a man who was controlling and kept me away from my mother. And the more distance there was, the harder it was to get back on track with her. Especially since I didn't want to face my problems with this man, and seeing my mother was like putting it right in my face. I couldn't admit I had done something so wrong and I began to think that I was useless.

"It took me a long time to realize it wasn't me, and that I had sacrificed my connections to my mother and brothers to appease him. But during that time, I was not protecting myself. My mother has always been so right about people and had such courage. Had she lived closer, I might have turned my life around sooner. Today I am back in touch with my mother because I am back in touch with myself. I can accept that she does know these things, that she is wise and motherly. And she can accept that I will never have her life and do what she did at the age of 40 or 45. Mostly I think she expected me to be stronger and to demand respect. That is how she has lived her life. But my existence can't be compared to hers. That's what we've both learned—no matter how she taught me to be."

If the family dynamic sets the stage for our future success in relationships and our childhood has been filled with discord, we often follow this path into our adulthood. All the while we are trying to distance ourselves, or to find a form of escape. The loss of family ties, to siblings or parents, is traumatic and disturbing, yet circumstances can facilitate women becoming physically, if not emotionally, reconnected to their mothers. There is a population of daughters who find themselves nursing an ill mother or sister as years pass. If the two women have not reconciled their differences, there is an underlying resentment despite the situation. The old unresolved pattern re-emerges between mother and daughter or sisters, and the old patterns repeat themselves. It is only if the woman is able to shift her perception and to clearly see the entire picture then there is a chance to change. If not, these women as caregivers may use inertia intentionally, as a survival mechanism. They function at a low level, to get through the ordeal, without being invested emotionally. The mother and daughter must make a concerted effort to reconnect.

ILLNESS AND RECONCILIATION

If a mother is ill and her daughter comes to care for her, this does not negate a family history. If a daughter is ill and her mother comes to care for her, this also does not negate a family history. It is a process for the two women to heal their relationship.

Women in midlife are stressed because of the simultaneous demands of caring for children as well as aging parents. And women are dealing with their own psychic issues involving the transition to middle age. The support system she has set up–those of her social network and family ties–are her own defense against poor health. These positive reinforcements provide positive measures for women dealing with aging parents.

Clarissa, at 49, has been caring for her ill mother for the past ten years.

"The hardest part was those first few years, when my daughter was small and I had no one to leave her with. She would have to go with me to the hospital and it became a part of our life experience. As a child I had watched my mother care for her mother, and now I was caring for her. She had open-heart surgery and we were there for her and afterward, for her recovery.

"My mother and I were already close but this really changes things. At some point I became the adult and my mother became the child. Had I been there full time, I might have resented it, but my brother and sister were there too, to some extent. It is pretty difficult to get those calls where you have to drop everything and run to the hospital. But it also becomes a part of your life. That was how I became the one in charge—it was cemented over time, as I made the decisions about her health care. I was the one making sure she was getting the right kind of drugs and that she was comfortable in her hospital room. It seems a long time ago since she was taking care of me when I had the chicken pox."

It is a testimony to the gendered bond that mothers, daughters and sisters, despite their dissimilar styles and lives, will come to each other's aid. These scenarios are the direst of all, and the experience acutely affects one's senses. The result of dealing with an ill mother, sister or friend can be life-altering. The ability to heal family relationships and friendships, or to recreate them on terms acceptable to both parties, is the obvious goal. It is by understanding our own strength that we come to recognize the strength in others. This enables us to choose a positive method of approach for these intricate connections—or to disengage, if necessary.

SISTERS IN MIDLIFE

- **Sibling rivalry begins in childhood**
- **It plays out in adult siblings through a competition in lifestyle**
- **This could last a lifetime**

Nora, who at 40 is the oldest of three sisters and one brother, has been ambivalent toward one sister since childhood. "My sister, Sallie, who is three years younger than I am, has always been competitive with me. My twin sisters who are six years younger are another story altogether. We get along fine, but since they are twins, they are totally attached to each other. I am married with four children and Sallie is divorced without any children. I have always been considered the prettier sister and she has always resented that. I reach out to her and I always invite her over to see the children, but they think of her as ornery and cranky. It is complicated because I feel so responsible to this sister on some level. I suspect that one day I will be taking care of her. Once my parents go, I will be the one who watches over her. Her problem is that she is alone. I think it is very sad.

"One of the issues here is that my husband and she do not really get along. And since we live in the same place, it gets complicated on weekends when I feel badly and feel like I should invite her over. I know she is alone and we are altogether. But I also know it won't go that well once she comes over. I keep waiting for it to improve and I can't believe that this isn't possible. Maybe as we get older it will get better, because we will mellow."

Even in the closest of families, there can be sibling rivalry. Between sisters, this rivalry and competition escalates. In my book, *Sisters: Devoted or Divided*, the exploration of sisterhood includes sisters who are competitive, supportive, jealous, and exclusive. When sisters are a combination of competitive and supportive, much of it has to do with birth order. In Nora's case, she is the oldest of four siblings and feels that she is the protector on some level. Yet she and her sister who is closest to her age do not get along and the tension is heightened by lifestyle differences. While Nora hopes that as they get older the competition will decrease, there is also the possibility of the conflict becoming greater.

In some cases, sisters may become complete without other female friendships and their exclusivity as sisters will nourish them. Other times, the sibling rivalry will persist throughout adulthood. What is curious is how many siblings actually admit that they are embroiled in this ongoing condition, and how long it takes them to realize that it is unhealthy. When an adult woman does take a step back and understands her flawed relationship with a sibling, there is a chance to heal and go forward.

For sisters who have felt they were an invincible team, jealousy might not arise until one of them has an extreme change in circumstances. Lydia, who did not get married until the age of 38, recognizes how her marriage has affected her relationship with her sister.

"Once I got married," says Katja, "I saw how deep-seated Fanny, my sister's, jealousy was. Until then I really didn't know it. We were raised to believe we should protect each other, and still we fought like crazy when we were younger. I had this impression when I became a teenager, which I did first because I am eighteen months older, that Fanny actually wanted to be me. Then we finished college and we lived together as single women, as both sisters and friends. That was until I met Bill. Now Fanny, who lives in our old apartment, won't even call me and she resents my happiness. And I pretend that it isn't happening, so I can avoid any conflict, thinking it is better left alone. So I call her and I push and pull for us to be together, and it is very tense. Finally Fanny will agree and then we get together and pretend that everything is okay. During those visits, I feel like it could be okay. But I am beginning to face that nothing can be the same and that my sister can't move on in her own life.

"Part of the problem is how we were raised. We were taught to believe that everything was always fine. Being roommates and sisters seemed like a double protection against the world. Getting married made it complicated because not only did I lose touch with the relationship I had with my Fanny, but marriage is very difficult in its own right. I consider marriage to be a shakedown. Living with a partner is another story altogether. So when it comes to both Fanny and my new life, I make decisions based on what works best for me. That is my final analysis."

Like Katja, Patricia, at 45, also has had a built-in competition with her sister which she is presently dealing with.

"I blame so much of this on my parents. My sister is four years older and I was always the adoring little sister when we were small. I was never equal and my sister needed homage. Basically I worked so hard for her to love me that it reached the point where we were both adult women and I was still playing it that way. Then we were both married and she did not accept me as her equal. I knew it but I kept pretending it wasn't happening and expecting it to get better. The big problem became that I no longer wanted to look up to her.

"I didn't see why there should be the age difference should any longer be a factor at 30 and 34, at 40 and 44. And the competition over money began to be a big part of our relationship—as in whose husband made what and how did we live. The sick part was I kept trying to please her. Meanwhile, she was critical of me from the minute I walked into the room: I was too dressed up or I wasn't dressed properly—I could never win. Then we both had children, and there was a chance to raise our children as very close cousins. Recently her daughter became ill and I helped out in many ways. She was appreciative but cold at the same time. This was the last straw. Today I am keeping my distance and looking to my friends to be there for me." As so often is the case, when sisters are estranged or the relationship is rocky, they will seek out female friends to compensate.

Sisters who grew up in a family without brothers lack a certain masculine influence. Although they may not themselves realize it, they miss out on an opportunity of learning how to relate to men, and often lack confidence in dealing with them. Instead, they trade exclusively in the camaraderie of women, an extended sisterhood. Those who did grow up with sisters will exhibit characteristic behavior into middle age. Younger sisters are always looking for connections to older sisters. When they are not available, this can cause great pain. Often we also witness a negative triangle, where the eldest and youngest sister bond and persistently exclude the middle sister, perhaps irrevocably. But adulthood brings a maturity that can help overcome childhood rivalries between sisters. There is an opportunity to reach out and become friends with a sister with whom one was never close before. They can become an unexpected source of insight and support.

Brothers and sisters have a competition that is different from the sister–sister rivalry but stems from the same source, the family. Brothers and sisters may get disconnected–the rivalry may be so intense that any relationship, let alone friendship, between them may seem no longer possible. Like any other human beings, they develop and become their own persons with discrete interests, professions, and of course, geography. Politics, friends, profession, may also exert an influence.

Studies as recent as the past ten years, such as those conducted by Shapiro in 1995 and Lips in 1995, indicate that parents treat their infant sons differently than they treat their infant daughters. Brothers and sisters raised in the same family have distinct expectations placed upon them. A household where the parents engage in a nontraditional, non-gendered form of childrearing may still want their sons to be aggressive. Daughters will have dolls while sons will be given sports paraphernalia.

The "invisible" work of housekeeping begins early for girls/sisters and the message that boys/brothers do not have to bother with this is conveyed at an equally early age. However, these gendered responsibilities and messages do not alleviate competition. Being the favorite child is now extended not only to birth order but sex. Many women, years later, confess that they felt inferior to their older brother, or younger brother, because her parents favored a son over a daughter. The theory that a male sibling has more freedom and more opportunity dies hard, even in today's world, where we are halfway there, and look to a future of nonsexist young parents raising enlightened children. If a woman is acutely aware of deficiencies in her own upbringing in terms of siblings and gender, hopefully she has taken these lessons to heart. Her daughters and sons, then, will not be favored by gender, and not treated so unequally because of their sex. Instead each will be tended to according to individual personality and individual need.

CROSSING GENDER LIVES

- **Sibling rivalry begins in childhood**
- **It plays out in adult sibling relationships**
- **This could last a lifetime**

"I do not speak to my younger brother," Loretta, aged 39, tells us. "When I see him we are cordial to each other, but too much happened in our childhood for us to maintain a relationship independent of holiday dinners. My brother is a very successful attorney and there was a time when our father needed his help. That was when I realized that I was the one calling him all the time and he would never call me back. I was the one who was galvanizing his efforts; he wasn't forthcoming on his own. But because he is the son and the only boy out of three children, my father praised him to the sky. I suppose I couldn't bear it anymore and so I did two things. I lost any energy I had for him, and I began to look the other way, like I wasn't there for him. That was the only way to get through.

"It wasn't so hard to get away with this kind of avoidance because my brother lives far away and he is very busy. We do not have similar lives or a similar set of values. He sees me with my kids, without a career, and he judges. Meanwhile, I wasn't raised to have a career, he was. So there is no personal interplay anymore. My mother makes it a command performance and we all show up for certain yearly events such as Christmas. But my brother's perspective on life and mine are not the same. He is in his own world and I am in mine. Just because we are related doesn't mean we are the same and have the same goals and values. It has taken me years to get to the point where I feel justified in my life and where my brother's judgments can be ignored. That's how I do it, by ignoring him to an extent. To me that is being in touch with myself."

Achievement is often an area of competition between brothers and sisters. A woman who achieves more than her brother may be upsetting the expectations inherent in a traditional family. When a sister/woman does excel, she is acutely aware of what the odds are, not only in the workplace, but within her own family structure.

"My brothers were taught to excel and my sisters and I were taught to get by," says Abigail, who at 38 is a partner in an accounting firm. "No one even considered me a possibility for a serious job. Then it turned out that my father needed more family members in the family business and since I had a business degree, I was asked in. I stayed there for ten years and then I knew I had to get out because I hated it. I disliked being with my father and brothers–they were so sexist. I knew that I had the right skills and that I could make more money elsewhere. So I left and started fresh, without any connections, just my own abilities. And that is where I am today. I think that everyone resents me, it is not gender specific. My mother thinks I should have stayed with the family business because that is her fantasy. My brothers can't believe I'm doing well, and my sisters have no career, since they took my mother's advice."

LOST ILLUSIONS

Realizing our problems and then distancing ourselves from unhealthy family situations is a way of preserving ourselves.

One of the common myths is that we must get along because we are born into the same family, and that anything short of this is a failed relationship. The hope is to heal any rift that existed in childhood, and to stop acting as rivals and more like adults. Once a woman understands what has transpired between herself and a family member, there are compromises to be made. More significantly, it is when we understand our own needs that we can work through family issues. As Judith Orloff explains in her book, *Intuitive Healing: 5 Steps to Physical, Emotional and Sexual Wellness*, "Your belief matters… What anybody else says is right for you is irrelevant if you don't feel it yourself. We often go years mesmerized by a litany of illusions about who we are—from the media or our parents—that we must unlearn." If we apply this approach to our relationship with family members, it will allow us to ease up. Then we can establish whatever successful relationship is possible, even if it requires more distance, for us to feel honest and awake—to avoid repeating our past.

9

Confusion in our Careers/Financial Sleep

"It was very difficult for me to find a path with my career," Isabelle, age 48, admits, "because I have been given mixed messages by the media and the marketplace. While I have a law degree and I have practiced off and on, it has always been a career which comes second to my role as mother and wife. I was encouraged to look at Gloria Steinem and consider her a role model. But how could I, when her message wasn't clear to me? Were we to turn our backs on our children and those responsibilities, or were we supposed to believe that we could have it all? I tried to do it all–but being housewife, career woman and mother was virtually impossible. It simply caught up to me.

"I took several years off and I tried to sort it out. Then I was hired by a brand-new events office not too far from my home. I did it while the children were at school and I became very successful. So the life I led, of a suburban wife and mother, has been altered, not only by a divorce, but by this incredible career which has unexpectedly developed. Another way of getting myself back was by having this job, by saying to myself and the world that I could do it. So while I might not look as good as I did ten years ago, I feel much stronger, much better. And I see myself as leading a life much different than my mother's. Eventually, I was able to go beyond the way I was brought up and do what was best for me."

There are few venues as dominated by the patriarchal mindset as the workplace. Therefore, great fortitude is required for women to achieve in their careers, with or without a family at home. Sixty-four million women are in the workforce today, however, according to the U.S. Census Bureau, and more American women are self-supporting than ever before. Thus it is obvious that tremendous strides have been made. Yet the bias persists, and the glass ceiling has not disappeared. For those women who have devoted their lives to their careers, it can be devastating when there is a setback. For those who have bought into the fiction that our gender is equal and anything is possible, they now question their work and the commitment made to it. At this point, some women may disengage from their career to reevaluate their path. Simultaneously, others may pursue a career after years of commitment to home and mothering.

Although women have been taught that they have multitask efficiency, the reality of a full-time career combined with the obligations of motherhood can be daunting. Once again, it is the babyboomer who agonizes over this. It is she who is afflicted with the consequences of sustaining a balance between career and home life. While men have been allowed to focus in one direction at one time, women are spread thin and yet expected to be effective. Finally, in many situations, it becomes too wearing. The "Happiness Flash" column in the November 2000 column of *SELF* Magazine asked the question, "Do Men Need Mommies?" The answer is that when wives worked over forty hours a week, their husbands' health declined. If the women worked fewer hours, their husbands' health did not decline. The research indicates that husbands are kept healthy by "having wives around." "Oh, please," reads the blurb, "who keeps an eye on us?!" To further complicate matters, men do not like to betray dependency on women. Susan Faludi explains why this is the case in her book, *Stiffed: The Betrayal of the American Man*. Not only are men not permitted to appear dependent, but they can't be oppressed because they are understood to be the oppressors. American women, on the other hand, Faludi says, "were strangely diminished and demoralized by new mass culture." They become overwhelmed and confusion sets in, clouding their vision and causing them to settle.

The traditional non-paying job of mothering and housekeeping, which is considered "invisible work," has always been considered less worthy than work that is performed outside the home, in the "real world." This discouraging concept is juxtaposed to the working woman who emerged in the 1970s, a woman without any role models to emulate and little training for the constant tension between family or spouse and a career. In a very recent occurrence, these women have acknowledged their predicament, shed the constraints of too much responsibility, and questioned the demands placed upon them. Thus the cultural message of the seventies and eighties is now being defied. This is fortunate for the next generation of women, who have more opportunities and better-acclimated husbands because of their own take on the situation. Hopefully they will benefit from the babyboomers' trial and error.

As MacDermid, Heilbrun, and DeHaan note in their essay "Employed Mothers in Multiple Roles," a woman's generativity has been identified with mothering for so long that it isn't easy to imagine other contexts. The authors point out that "adult role systems become more complex and diverse," and parenthood becomes "less predominant." The "discontinuities" in women's lives are quite apparent, as they take on the role of "worker, student and caregiver." The discarded dreams of women who married in the middle to late seventies and became inveterate mothers and wives, can now, in fact, be revisited.

It would be unfair to view motherhood as the only obstacle to women achieving their goals in their careers. The socialization of women is a slowly evolving process, with gender lines clearly drawn. What women have today is not total equality, but a closer approximation. This seems to have had an effect on younger women, from the ages of 25 to 35, who have grown up with more independence, and whose mothers, in their empty quest for role models, taught them what to be and what not to be. Their own diffidence sent their daughters a negative lesson–to have clarity, goals, and boundaries. Out of the "sleep" of women in their late 30s to mid-50s, their daughters born after 1980 come forth in charge of their own future in a way their mothers never were. What these younger women choose to do with their choices remains to be seen. What is evident however, is that they do not feel about their lives as their mothers did about theirs.

IMPLICIT MESSAGE

- **The lack of choice for women has somewhat abated**
- **The determination to have equal pay for equal work continues**
- **Out of their mothers' confusion, the way is paved for the daughters**
- **They will not make the same mistakes or sacrifices as their mothers**

The role conflict for women who are 40 to 50 years old today has been poignant and mitigated only by the changing responsibilities of their convention-bound lives. In other words, time, which is threatening, is also a great equalizer. A woman who gave up her career in 1980 to raise her first child, and subsequently had two more babies, now has college-age and teenage children. She is able and ready to reenter the work force–a form of self-renovation. Conversely, a woman of this age group who did not have children but pursued her career path may suffer a deep regret that she did not raise a family.

This sentiment, coupled with the stresses of the work world which she has endured–including sexism in many fields–leaves her drained and without the position she deserves.

Denise, who at the age of 46, has decided to put all of her energy into her career, had no role model in her mother or her contemporaries.

"My mother never worked a day of her life," Denise says, "because it wasn't expected of her. She had worked until she married my father and once we were raised, they retired together and moved out west. My father, who is a very kind man, was so strict in the roles that he and my mother played that she never wore trousers, let alone jeans. If someone's mother worked, it indicated a problem, a desperate measure this woman had taken, putting her children at risk. This attitude was never discussed but alluded to. Mealtime and weekends and after-school time were serious matters in our family. My sister and I did exactly as we were told.

"I married right out of college and I got a job at a school. I was encouraged to teach but it was always understood that I was just waiting to begin a family. And I bought into the whole picture too, because I didn't see anything else being offered up, and because even my husband had no other vision. The women's movement did not escape me, but it seemed to take place on another planet. While I admired it, it was not my reality. When I was married for three years, I had my first child. That was when my fate was sealed. I loved my baby, but I felt I was a prisoner in my own life. I would walk her early in the morning down the city streets to watch people rushing to get to work. I had always loved having to be somewhere, having a purpose in the form of a job. I had imagined I'd be in school administration one day.

"Twenty years later, my eldest child is off at college and I am teaching part time. I do curtail my schedule so that it works for my daughter who is in junior high school. It is important I get to work and get to do my mothering too."

Women who return to the work force after their children are grown, according to sociologist Alice Michaeli, are still concerned about their job as mother and wife. "The concept of work is that it can revolve around the children's and husband's schedule," Michaeli explains. It has been impressed upon them their entire lives to accommodate others. These women may do something of interest but it cannot conflict with their primary responsibility. "Women who worked while waiting to be married and have children were not geared toward the independence of women five to ten years younger than they are," says Michaeli. "They might have worked off and on during their lives, to supplement their husband's income, to help out in the office, or as temporary condition. The motivation, for most of these women, is not to establish a career, but to remain on the 'mommy track' and 'family track'."

The cultural legacy of man as principal breadwinner in a family and women as responsible to their house, husband and children endures because it is at the center of our lives. Whether we conform to the plan or break free, the expectation has colored our behavior and our choices or our lack thereof. Mary Ann LaManna and Agnes Riedmann's textbook *Marriages and Families* describes the ways that the role of the family wage

233

earner has changed in America. Despite these strides, the main/secondary provider couple where the husband works and the wife takes care of the house, is still considered the default, compared with the idea of the "co-provider couple," where the woman is equally responsible financially, or the "ambivalent provider couple," where the wife's provisions are not completely defined, and finally the "role-reversed couple," where the husband stays at home with the child and the wife works and makes the money.

The number of women in the labor force has grown tremendously in the last 100 years, and the results have been most dramatic in the past thirty years. According to Lamanna and Riedmann, in 1997 almost two-thirds of women with children under the age of six were paid employees. The U.S. Census reports that in 1997, 59 percent of white married mothers and 69.5 percent of black married mothers of children under the age of one were a part of the labor force. The employment rate for Latina women in 1997 rose to 55 percent.

STATISTICS FOR WORKING MOTHERS

The U.S Census reports that by the late 1990s:

- **59% of White Married Mothers were a part of the work force**

- **69.5% of Black Married Mothers were a part of the work force**

- **55% of Latina Women were part of the work force**

Gloria, who at 54 has worked the last fifteen years in the same position, considers her work to be a financial means to an end.

"I have been in housekeeping in the same hotel for so long that I've become very comfortable with it. I am a single black mother with five children who are now grown. But I when I began here, they were all at home and I worked for one reason—I needed money to pay bills and a mortgage. I didn't think about a career but it was an eye-opener. I had been in places where I was made to feel like less and that really showed me something. Once I learned, I chose this job because I knew they were nice to women and it wasn't a place where men were better paid for the same work. I am proud of my job and I have known the women I work with and some of the clients for a long time. I believe I am a role model for my girls, who see that I am independent because I make my own money and I could support our family.

"I have always told my girls it is important to work and be on their own. I feel lucky to have this job because it has been mine for so long. Maybe I would have been paid better somewhere else, but I know how they treat minorities here and that counts to me. My daughters respect this about me, but they want more. They want real careers, not just a job. Once I'm out of the hotel, I'm not thinking about it, I am finished for the day. My oldest daughter describes her work in the field of television and she can't escape it. It's with her all the time. This is a different generation, but I still know I planted the seed. I remind my girls it is a man's world and to pay attention. It took me a few years to understand how true that is and I wanted them to know from the get-go. Maybe I needed money, but I also learned the hard way that women have to do for themselves."

In a survey by PARENTS magazine in 1996, 61 percent of mothers reported that they would like a part-time position. Yet according to the 1998 U.S. Bureau of Labor Statistics, under a quarter of working women do have part-time work. The part-time mother is considered more convention-bound and is obviously more available to her children than a full-time working mother. The common pattern for married couples is for the wife to work until she has children and to return to work once her children are older. What makes this so difficult is the pressure to build a career by one's early thirties. This negates any opportunity for a woman who returns ten or fifteen years later and resumes a career which was suspended so long before.

These women have lost precious time and skills, as dramatized on a recent episode of *Once and Again*, the Lifetime series on divorce, single parents, romance and children. When Sela Ward's character, Lily Manning, returns to work after years at home with her two daughters, she finds herself answering to a boss who appears to be fifteen years her junior. Her work etiquette is rusty and she is awkward with the computer. Over time, Lily adapts to the work world and adjusts to its innovations. Supporting her bold leap is her boyfriend Rick's mother, who visits one Thanksgiving. This possible future mother-in-law lauds Lily for her bravery, explaining how ill-equipped she was to deal with work and financial responsibility when she found herself a single mother.

Joanne, who at 48 is a mother of three college-age children, worked part time until two years ago. At that point she returned to school to complete her nursing degree. Today she works on a children's ward in a local hospital.

"I see work as an escape and as a way of understanding myself. I now find myself immersed in the hospital and it keeps me from thinking of my life and my responsibilities. Although I'm glad that I raised my children first, before I sought this career, I also know I wouldn't want to be home any more. I would have felt guilty if I did this earlier, but I love that I have established myself for now and for the future.

"What I love about nursing is that it has a beginning and an end. I am expected to be there at a certain time and when I leave, it is over until the next day. I am very attached to the children in the ward and I can't believe what they go through, but I also know that my connection to them is in shifts. With my children and my husband, there are no shifts. There were days when all I did was drive the kids back and forth, and make meals. Now I have a life that is all mine."

Like Joanne, Ellen in her early forties realized she wanted a career. "My father had always discouraged me from having a full-time job and for years I worked in my husband's office part time. He is an accountant with long hours and I helped with the bookkeeping. I never felt that this was a career—it was another definition of me as someone else—in this case, Rick's wife. In my other hat I was Deidre or Jack's mother. I saw the time spent at Tom's office as a way to help him out, but I felt like a clerk, not like I was establishing a career.

"Ironically, it was my husband who suggested I go back to school. I wanted to do something that was all mine. I had gone into the marriage knowing I wanted children before I was 30 and suddenly I was looking at the other side of my life. I wanted to do something constructive that was just for me. It took years for me to become aware of my own needs. As I saw my kids growing up, I wondered what I would do for myself. I explored different careers popular with women, and in the end decided on teaching administration, which is another form of caregiving. It works for me, and I am pleased that I took myself to another level. It has been very gratifying."

These are impressive strides for women, and the improvement has been undeniably steady and significant. Yet there are obstacles to success. It is these very obstacles which cause women to be in denial in their careers, and to accept less than optimal conditions. Feminist Historian Gerda Lerner reminds us in her book, *The Creation of the Feminist Consciousness,* that this means that women know they belong to a subordinate group, and because of this they have anguished. This "condition of subordination is not natural, but societally determined." Lerner writes that the women have had a longstanding economic dependence upon men, which is one of the many impediments to their raised consciousness.

Since our society has motivated men to compete for positions, the advent of women qualified for the same place was not universally welcomed. Discrimination against women persists—thus unequal pay for equal work. According to the U.S.

Bureau of Labor Statistics in 1998, women receive 77 cents for every dollar that men earn in the same position. But often the careers that appeal to women are not those which pay well, and are called "pink-collar jobs." According to the U. S. Bureau of the Census, in 1998 only 14 percent of women filled managerial positions. Yet 24 percent of women were in administrative support jobs, including clerical work. The difference in careers for men and women is called "occupational segregation," and while there has been a steady improvement in the past twenty years, women continue to fill the bulk of the lower-paying vocations. The salient question is—are they aware of this, and simply willing to take less, or is our society structured so that the occupations which entice women are traditionally lower paying because women accept sub-optimal conditions?

PINK-COLLAR JOBS AND WOMEN

In 1998, according to the U. S. Census Bureau, 14% of managerial positions were filled by women. 24% of administrative support jobs were filled by women. The improvement in placement of women in the work force is slow but steady.

The delicate balancing act of wife and working woman only exacerbates the problem of inequality. When women work full time, their second shift becomes that of wife and/or mother. As sociologist Alice Michaeli views it, the roles are now blurred.

"What careers have done for women is put them in a crunch. We cannot fault men because of the lack of socialization for us and the lack of role models. Women have been in training to be wives and mothers since birth. Women today are very tired."

An up-to-the-minute depiction of the sharp contrast between the working woman and the pampered, non-working wife can be seen in the recent film, *Dr. T & the Women*, starring Richard Gere. The film takes place in Dallas, where spoiled, elegant women lunch, shop, and dress. Dr. T (Gere) is their gynecologist, who recognizes each and every woman as special. Yet as much as he adores his beautiful, non-working wife, played by Farrah Fawcett, he cannot save her from a fate which seems to stem from boredom and benign neglect. Fawcett's character retreats to childhood because, her psychologist explains, she is loved too much. When Helen Hunt appears, playing a younger woman, a single, independent golf pro who believes men are sport, Dr. T. is beguiled. Both his wife and his lover are extremes; it would take a blend of these two characters to come up with the perfectly balanced, self-aware, cherished woman with a career.

Monique made a conscious decision in her work and consequently was able to navigate a path effectively. "I am fifty years old and I have been working since college and had summer jobs before that. I have always been drawn to my career and I was raised in the world of advertising. What I find interesting is that years ago, men dominated the business and now there are plenty of women in the field. Fifteen years ago women who were producers were paid less but that has improved somewhat. This industry is really a fraternity, with golf games and drinks at the club. There are still very few women at the top.

"My way of surviving was just to do my job. At times I wished I could be more like a man, and have more manly qualities. Men relate differently to each other and speak another language. I saw men shutting me out and I knew I couldn't fight it. It isn't that I wanted to be a man, I just wanted the advantage that is available to men. Because there were no women in this industry who I could look up to, I had to make my own way. I went through the motions of being a pet to the men when I was very young. I was very fortunate though because I knew I had to grow up, and make the next leap to a substantial place.

"I believe I did all of this to prove to my father how good I was. I certainly didn't want to emulate my mother, who had given up her career to raise us. I simply could not respect her choice. I saw my mother as someone who could become hysterical with five kids to raise. I felt I was more connected to my father and I wanted to be like him because he was not frustrated like my mother. Today, years later, I can finally relate to my mother and what she went through. But I did not want to listen to her when I was younger. So I followed my father in my career but found my own niche and it has been rewarding."

There is a great advantage for those women who are able to establish their own requirements in the workplace and who have a clear understanding of where their work fits into their lives. While it obviously takes time and determination to achieve this heightened awareness, it is a path to finding oneself. Tending to the needs of the family and looking to the man as provider has become a diminished ideal for these women. The fiction of taking care of everyone else, which has persisted for centuries, has exhausted modern-day women who now have other aspirations. "The idea of being a 'nice girl' is no longer so meaningful to women," Dr. Ronnie Burak tells us. "There are women who have given up a dream of a career to subjugate themselves to a husband. Others have a job while waiting for something to happen, and end up finding their career later on. Although the dream stays buried in some instances, in many cases these women realize they need to pursue it and the dream reemerges."

EITHER/OR

- **Women who devote themselves to work might negate other areas of their lives**
- **Homemakers feel they are missing the career boat**
- **There is little middle ground**

For Althea, who is a general surgeon, having a young child is only a part of the challenge of being a female in her field. At the age of 35, she has been engrossed in her career for eight years.

"I see medicine as a male-dominated profession and filled

with the old-boys school mentality. But for me, this exposure has made me stronger. I did my job and I got through medical school, my internship and residency knowing it was this way. I have been motivated to be a physician since I was very young. Both my parents are doctors, and that was what inspired me. My mother was a good role model by her education, but she resented that her career did not go as far as it could have because of her children. And I saw that my father pushed my brothers but not me to become a doctor. Then he saw me breeze through the education and he was proud of me.

"I suppose I had something to prove. I am tougher and stronger than my brothers, which was very surprising to our family. My career is a part of me, and I do the best I can in my profession. It is tied into my psyche and it compels me. My friends do not feel this way about their professions. Now I have a small son, and I have altered my schedule to be there for him. My mother, who was denied her chance to move ahead in her career, wasn't really there for me, although she thought she was. So I have decided to make myself available to my son and also be true to myself with my work."

Many of Althea's friends who have small children do not work.

"We were all conditioned to think we could work and have babies. Then I look around at all of my friends, who are 35-year-old mothers do not want to work. A part of it is the kind of careers they have—such as law or working for a corporation. Those jobs are demanding in a way that wouldn't allow them to make their own schedules. Women my age view the decision not to work as a luxury. I just question if they were planning ahead as I did. I don't think having children is an excuse not to work, not to do both. I was always certain that I'd get to this level but it required a great deal of independence."

Not all women have the education and options which Althea has had, and her diligence notwithstanding, she is a part of the 53 percent of working women who find themselves in male-dominated careers. Although Veronica's situation differs from Althea's, both have had to navigate their own path to success.

"I have been working my entire life and I have been a single mother for thirteen years. At first I was a teacher's aid, then I became an administrative assistant because it had better benefits. In both jobs I had to think about when I could see my son and what hours would be best for us. I have thought that men have the upper hand in the office but I did not see it as much when I worked in the schools. I have pushed myself to get ahead because no one else could have pushed me. Having been in the second job for three years, I am quite aware of how minorities and women are treated. It isn't fair that men think they deserve more than women. I put up with this because I need the money and because I can get ahead in this office. That is why I stay here.

"It has always been stressful to ask friends to look after my child if I am working late. When he was smaller, I worried about him while I was at work and on days when he was sick, I really panicked. And there were times when I was scheduled to work at night, serving at parties, to make some extra money, and I had to cancel because the sitter didn't show up. Being a black woman complicates it, so I try not to think about that, and to stay focused on what opportunities there are for me. I remember how hard my mother worked and my father wasn't there. I really thought I'd have a husband and father for my child—and that I would be a good wife, who only worked part time."

A good wife, by traditional standards, is someone who takes care of the home and has little aspiration beyond this. The children are taken care of and the household hums. She may work part time, knowing that her job is not central to the finances of the marriage. She might even spend her wages to pay for day care, thus utilizing her job as a way to escape the confines of household duties. She is supposed to be amicable and pleasant at all times.

The new generation of women, both single and married, has an outlook which encompasses a greater world. The options open to this generation include the chance to float in and out of work, the chance to marry and raise a family—or not. For these women, whatever their marital status, work may not be the only motivation in their lives. This differs from men, who continue to define themselves by their professions.

POINT OF VIEW

Today women between the ages of 30 and 40 view work as one option in their lives. Men, on the other hand, continue to seek self-definition through their careers.

At the age of 32, Alex has decided not to pursue a career. Married with two children, she devotes her time to her family.

"I have never really established myself in terms of work. I was married very young the first time and I was still in school. After my divorce I finished graduate school and worked for two years as a social worker and then I married again. In this marriage we had children right away, and I have not worked at all.

"I do not regret not working, nor do I view it as if I am missing something. Maybe I just don't pay enough attention to how I'll feel later, but for now, I do not feel pressured to have a career. Maybe when my children begin school I will suddenly look around and have regrets. My mother is a workaholic and is totally committed to her career. Yet when we were younger, she only worked part time. I think the difference is that she was waiting to begin this part of her life, to make up for lost time—and I'm not like that at all. I also want to be with my children while they are small and then I'll develop my career. My husband is in favor of this plan too. If I can afford to at home with the children and not have to contribute to our family monetarily, why not?

"The other factor for me is that my mother lives three thousand miles away and I have no support system in an extended family. I have friends who work part time or full time, but their mothers and mothers-in-law are around to be with the children. They can at least check up on them during the day while the kids are with sitters. In my situation I will be in my late thirties when our family is finished growing and I'm ready to go to work. I want a big career then, in the entertainment field. And at that age I will have a good chance to make it happen. My mother was always an excellent role figure. If I am half as successful as she has become, I'll feel that I've accomplished something."

An article entitled "The New-Economy Family" by Nancy Ann Jeffreys, published in *The Wall Street Journal* in the fall of 2000 focuses on the classic high-powered two-career couple who have returned to the "Old Family." The husband/father works and the wife/mother remains at home, in these cases because the husband is successful enough that it doesn't obligate both partners to work. Not surprisingly, the spouse whose income has skyrocketed is the husband's—but the nonworking wife is not quite the stereotype of the 1950s model. Instead she is someone who voluntarily forgoes a successful career for her children, and husband.

Yet this return to the traditional family is not stress-free for women. Some couples interviewed by Jeffreys found the arrangement satisfactory, making wives/mothers much more available to their husbands and children than they would otherwise be had they remained in their jobs. Others were conflicted, with the wives missing their own income and planning to return to work when the children got older. Categorically, the one-income family is becoming a trend in certain financial circles. The Federal Reserve Board reports that in the past two years almost half of those families whose income is between $250,000 and $500,000 has a sole breadwinner, whereas six years earlier the proportion was 38 percent.

SOLE BREADWINNERS

- **Women give up excellent careers to raise a family**
- **The Federal Reserve Board reports that in almost half of families earning $250,000 to $500,000 only the husband works**
- **Wives of these men might plan to return to work in later years**

Kelly, who is 33, has made the decision to put off her career in favor of marriage. Her husband's work schedule has required that he travel often. Because she is not working, she is able to go with him.

"I attended school on scholarship and I have an MBA. I'm not working right now and that was part of the deal when I got married. At present I am willing to wait to go back to work, until the right time in terms of my husband's career. I was raised to know I could be anything I wanted and that I would succeed. I was encouraged to get a degree first, and education was very important to both my parents. I was taught by my mother to have my own career and not to depend on a man. So while I 'm in a marriage where I am subjugating myself on some level for my husband's profession, I don't see it as all negative. I have women friends who are ten years older who think I'm crazy, who warn me I'll be regretful.

"We do not plan to have children and settle in one place,

but I keep thinking since I'm not working maybe we should have a child. But that was not the plan or the focus, and I see my friends who have babies as leading more limited lives. Some of them like to get away from their children and still work full time. Others work part time.

"These friends confess that they do not want to be trapped, nor do they want to fall behind. They say that their work gives them self-esteem. When we all get together, those who work are quick to define themselves that way. I feel content for now because my life with my husband is very exciting. And I am in a field where I can't work part time; I'm not an artist or freelance writer. I am trained to be an investment banker and it is more demanding."

Women have been prepared at any age to search for balance in their lives, negotiating husbands, households, and careers. And there could be other pursuits beyond work that do not necessarily entail a family. Brenda Szulman, psychotherapist, notes that women moving from their late thirties to forty are nearing a milestone. "In my practice I see a recurring theme. There are those women who are single and under 40 who are expected to work and do not have to be married. But when a women hits 40 and remains single, people begin to wonder if she has intimacy issues. It is as if she has lost her chance to become part of a couple at 40. For those women in their thirties who have a laissez-faire attitude about work, it may be that they are anxiety-ridden because they have not fulfilled the right slot, that of having a mate and maybe a child. They've only succeeded at their careers."

SHIFTING PRIORITIES

- **Women see themselves as building a career in their thirties**
- **By 35 women begin to worry about marriage**
- **Somewhere between 35 and 40, a family or mate may be more attractive than a career**

In Danielle's situation, a career is beginning to pale in terms of priorities, and the search for a partner is taking on more significance. At the age of 35, Danielle sees many of her peers enduring the same shift in balance.

"I have been working ever since college and today I have a very good job in the design department of a publishing house. Growing up my number one role model was my mother. When I began kindergarten, she returned to school to finish her degree. My mother was raised by my widowed grandmother and since there were three sisters, it was a matriarchal household. My grandmother was the only full-time working mother in their town. My mother, who is 59, and her sisters, who are older, are very strong women who have influenced me greatly.

"I was influenced by my family and also by a mentor at my first job. She was the VP of a company and she taught me how to approach the work world. She showed me how to act, dress and present myself. She was a single woman who had never married and her life was her work. So while I wasn't discouraged from marrying by my mother and her sisters, there was a message here that this could happen to someone and that a career could take over one's life. If that happened, it would be a lonely, stressful life. This was a warning to me, to make sure I find both—a profession that I enjoy, and a partner. Having had these role models has helped me. And now that I am 35, I'm beginning to think that work is not everything. I can do a good job and still have plenty left over for the rest of my life."

While the dilemma looms large for women and there is no easy solution, clearly the perfect goal would be to have both—a partnership and a satisfying career. In this ideal state, those couples with children would share the responsibilities of raising them. For the 70 percent of working women between the ages of 35 and 44, the dream dies hard. Yet according to the September 2000 issue of the Harvard Women's Health Watch newsletter, the 56 percent increase in the female working population in the past 50 years positions women to face the same work hazards as men. Because women fill high-powered jobs as well as part-time or 'pink-collar' jobs, they are at their job for more time than their predecessors. This, the Harvard Women's Health Watch reports, causes "occupational stress, where work conditions overwhelm our adaptive capabilities and make us sick in some way."

Women report more stress and stress-related illness than do men. This is because, as discussed earlier in this chapter, women strain in their numerous roles as employee, wife, housekeeper and caregiver for children and/or aging parents. It is interesting to note that women's stress hormones and blood pressure remain elevated even when the work day is completed, while this does not happen with men. Of course in our trying lives, stress has recently come into vogue, according to the *New York Times*. In June of 2000, the newspaper reported that people actually compete over how stressed out they feel. "Stress has become the badge of honor of the millennium," Arlene Kagley, psychologist, is quoted as saying. For women, this is not news, but a perennial aspect of their struggle and balancing act. What is newsworthy is how much more able women now are to admit the difficulties, to acknowledge how overloaded their lives feel. At some point women opt to make the necessary changes to lighten the load.

STRESS AND WOMEN

- **Women suffer from "occupational stress," where work conditions are overwhelming**

- **Women suffer more work-related illnesses than men**

- **Numerous roles for women contribute to stress**

- **It is advisable for women to simplify their lives**

Women who range from 30 to 40 are better able to balance their work, relationships, personal passions and interests than their older counterparts. It may be that they have a knowledge that women ten or twenty years their seniors do not have. Women who derive their sense of self from their husbands' position in the world do not aspire to careers of their own. Partly this is because their status will be upset. As Betty Carter notes in her essay "The Person Who Has the Gold Makes the Rules," "It is easy to overlook the dilemmas faced by these competent women because their affluence, or their husband's affluence, disguises their powerlessness." This, then is the other side of the argument, that these women are imprisoned by buying into the concept of being cared for. Their side of the bargain is that they will not abandon their family.

BALANCING ACTS: 30 to 39

- **These women can balance aspects of their lives**
- **They are independent**
- **They feel entitled**

vs. 40 to 45

- **This group felt they had to choose motherhood or work**
- **They do not feel independent**
- **Entitlement excludes them**

There is no question that times are changing. On June 22, 2000, the Wall Street Journal published an article by Christy Harvey "A Guide to Who Holds the Purse Strings." Harvey views women as the ones who make the decisions. According to the most recent Wall Street Journal/NBC News survey, "two-thirds to three-quarters of women say they are making many major economic decisions either independently or equally with a spouse." The promise of an equal work world is yet to be achieved, yet this study gives promise of a brave new world ahead. What seems clear is that women between the ages of 30 and 40 have another approach to the dilemma of profession versus home life. The shrill mantra of the late sixties which prevailed until the mid-eighties, that we can have it all, has resulted in a crash-and-burn for its constituency. Younger women do not intend to be overburdened by their responsibilities, but rather will make choices and bide their time. Their self-esteem and confidence in a future of right choices are impressive, mainly since the generation before them was so lacking in these qualities. Of course, so much of this depends upon a woman's heightened awareness and commitment to herself and her own personal goals.

10

Inheritance: Ourselves

Reclaiming ourselves is the culmination of a life change. Once a woman summons her courage and asks herself what her life is about, she is able to put her priorities in order. As demonstrated through introspective and personal journeys, women are more capable and talented than they sometimes know or believe. The heartfelt stories told in this book indicate that women no longer wish to be living a lie or feigning anything— in any area of their lives. In the anguish of reinventing ourselves, we come back to life. There are no more distractions; instead decisions are made based on self-knowledge with the intent of establishing ourselves in a healthy situation.

As Friedrich Nietzsche, the renowned philosopher, wrote in *The Will To Power*: "Very few manage to see a problem in that which makes our daily life, that to which we have long since grown accustomed—our eyes are not adjusted to it…" It is this very blindness, combined with centuries of conditioning, that makes it exceptionally challenging for women to re-sist, and ultimately disrupt, a life as they know it for a life that seems beyond their reach. What emerges in the multitude of stories told is a pattern of being asleep, or inert. This is fol-lowed by an anguished awakening, then often a return to sleep, and eventually a slow dawning or a sudden acknowledgment that this life one leads is not enough. An alternative has to be found.

Until now women have reacted out of fear and have re-mained in a bad place emotionally and physically for this very reason. Unable to let go, women have denied that there was any reason to change their lives or transform themselves. In the end, they can procrastinate no longer and must act now. A ten-year study conducted by the MacArthur Research Net-work on Successful Midlife Development found that the ma-jority of the population between the ages of 40 and 60 view midlife as a time of balance and fruitfulness. Perhaps the very idea that women can no longer put off the changes in their lives, but, because they are no longer 30 or 35, must act now, works in their favor.

I once overheard a conversation that deeply affected me. A woman was describing her parents, who were elderly, ill, and dying together in a local hospital, sharing the same room. Im-mediately upon entering the room, she saw and felt the aura they shared. It was that sensation that precipitated her own divorce, because it showed her what she would never have with her husband, and how deficient her marriage was. This story expresses my belief that self-discovery, even if we have been alienated from our own center, is not out of reach. Whatever the inspiration, we can always take repossession of ourselves and begin anew.

It isn't that one would have given up the experience of mothering or marriage, sisterhood, being a daughter, or a best friend. It is that we would have gone about it in another away and would have had a richer experience that comes with self-knowledge. It might not be that one would have not worked in a corporation had she known it was sexist. Rather, she would have handled it differently, and would have been prepared for the bias. When it comes to divorce, an affair or remarriage, it is only if we are truly in touch with our own moral center and know what we can and cannot abide that we will get through the experience. Then we become stronger, better—no longer asleep. We are awake instead of in denial. To have the courage to fix what doesn't work or to change what doesn't suffice, is not a trick or an art, but a capacity that comes from deep within. Author Eckhart Tolle in his book *The Power of Now* advises us that if we look too closely at the past, it will be endless. "You may think that you need more time to understand the past or become free of it, that the future will eventually free you of the past. This is a delusion. Only the present can free you of the past."

And so it seems especially true for women, who have spent precious years of their lives pleasing others and not heeding their inner voices. It is only when women know themselves that they can reach out to others in a positive fashion. The problem, of course, is how society interprets women and the cultural expectations that linger. Gender specialists have looked at the predicament of women, the faces we wear and the lives we lead–and the discrepancy between the two–and ascribe the fault to societal convention. The situation for women works both ways: a woman's emotional state is deeply affected by the roles she fills, and the roles she fills are deeply affected by her emotional state. "Spiritually a woman is better off if she cannot be taken for granted," Germaine Greer observed in *The Female Eunuch*, as long ago as 1970, when our collective consciousness was just starting to be raised.

Three decades later, we are still struggling to lay claim to our province. The more working mothers there are, the more they are accepted; the more single women there are, the more they are accepted. The more divorces, the more tolerance, the more that remarriage occurs, the less it is stigmatized, and so on. By reclaiming ourselves we create our own reality.

As I write this paragraph, my eye wanders to the coffee table, and I see that the February 2001 issue of MORE magazine's lead article reads "50 Ways to Reinvent Your Life." The fifty ways include a new career, skydiving, a new husband, liposuction, getting a facelift, changing religions, and fashioning a simpler existence. All of these efforts are laudable, but the hope is that twenty-five years from now this article–and this book–will seem obsolete, and the voices of the women and their dilemmas and social patterns will seem odd and perplexing. *Reclaiming Ourselves* will be merely a treatise on life as it once was lived. Yet how likely is this, really, when the writings of the feminist movement, from as many as thirty-five years ago, still make points as valid as those published in the year 2001? More worrisome is the fact that the recent adaptation to screen of *The House of Mirth*, a novel by Edith Wharton, applies today as a cautionary tale although it is set at the turn of the century.

The story dramatizes the sad plight of Lily Bart, a single woman who hasn't the foresight or proclivity to choose the "right" suitor. Lily is banned from society and denied an inheritance because she is both true to herself and at the same time sleepwalking through her life. By being true to herself she refuses to marry a man for money instead of love. In her sleepwalking mode, she invests her money unwisely with an unscrupulous man, trusting him to be honest. Both of these acts are reflected in her social fate. Lily is similar to women today in her confusion about what is expected of her. Her fall from grace reflects the inferior treatment of women and she is at a loss since she lacks the skills to make a living. Since Lily was expected to marry well, she has no recourse. Lily Bart represents a woman who awakens without options in the rigid society of 1907. What sets her plight apart from ours is that we have options.

Choices today allow women a variety of lifestyles and the mobility to leave one path for another, if necessary, with less reproach than in the past. It would be best if we could all simply make the right choices in our lives, guided by our own insights. The next-best route is to be responsible enough to face a mistake. Then we can leave the wrong choice, equipped to make the correct future choice in any and every aspect of our lives. This happens only when we are keenly conscious of our desires and intentions. At this juncture, we have taken our destinies into our own hands and have reclaimed ourselves.

In over 100 interviews, despite how disparate the stories, the one common theme I have heard is that of needing to work from the inside out. It is only the woman herself who is capable of making the change, and breaking free of the shackles that bind her. While the year 2001 is not perfect and women are certainly still considered the lesser sex, the progress is steady, if deliberate. For instance, a woman who yearns to have a baby today, even if she is 42 and single, has choices. The science is there, and society is slowly accepting of this category of mothers. As with any part of our lives, the rest is up to her.

A common thread throughout this project is how many women have allowed ten or twenty years to lapse before they have come to recognize their inner resources. By then they are deeply damaged. A healing process occurs simultaneously with the process of self-discovery. But society has still not completely encouraged women to have inner goals. We run from one superficial task to the next, feeling empty and forsaken. Time grows short as we approach our forties and there are no more excuses or procrastinations possible. Having been anesthetized for decades, the pain has been dulled, and we have been asleep, paralyzed into complacency. The woman who has fallen asleep is awakened by a cataclysmic event, and now faces the possibility of living a whole life, ripe with those challenges that come to those who participate fully.

The key to any scenario is that we create our own reality.

This is possible as long as we are awake and whole, ready to take on the risks and unafraid of what might seem perilous. *Reclaiming Ourselves: How Women Dispel a Legacy of Bad Choices* documents the discrepancies and gaps between all that women know intellectually and how we conduct our lives on a daily basis. The self-actualized, egalitarian way is not beyond our reach. It is time, at last, to reclaim ourselves and start anew.

References

Adler, Jerry. "Adultery: A New Furor Over an Old Sin," in Lamanna and Riedmann 2000.

Alcott, Louisa May. *Little Women*, Dover Publications, new edition, May 1997.

Allen, Jeffner, "Motherhood: The Annihilation of Women," in *Feminist Frameworks: Alternative, Theoretical Accounts of the Relations between Men and Women*, 3rd edition, edd. Alison Jaggar and Paula Rothenberg. New York: McGraw-Hill, 1993.

Angelou, Maya. *Wouldn't Take Nothing for My Journey Now*. New York: Random House, 1993.

Angier, Natalie. *Woman: An Intimate Geography*. New York: Anchor Books, 1999.

Antonucci, Toni, and Hiroko Akiyama. "Concerns with Others at Midlife: Care, Comfort or Compromise," in Lachman and James 1997.

Atwood, Margaret. *Cat's Eye*. New York: Doubleday, 1989.

Atwood, Margaret. *The Robber Bride*. New York: Doubleday, 1993.

Barash, Susan Shapiro. *Second Wives: The Pitfalls and Rewards of Marrying Widowers and Divorced Men*. Far Hills NJ: New Horizon Press, 2000.

Barnes, Michael L. and Robert J.Sternberg, edd., *The Psychology of Love*. New Haven: Yale University Press, 1988.

References

Benjamin, Jessica. *The Bonds of Love*. New York: Pantheon Books, 1988.

Bernard, Jessie, cited in Lamanna and Riedmann 2000.

Borysenko, Joan. *A Woman's Book of Life: The Biology, Psychology and Spirituality of the Feminine Life Cycle*. New York: Berkeley Publishing Group, 1996.

Boyle, William Antonio. "Sibling Rivalry and Why Everyone (and not only parents) Should Care About This Age-Old Problem." 1999/2000 www.angelfire.com.

Brady, Judy. "I Want a Wife," in *Complements*, edd. Anna Katsavos and Elizabeth Wheeler. New York: McGraw-Hill, 1995.

Bronte, Charlotte. *Jane Eyre*. New York: Signet, rev. and updated edition, 1997.

Caminiti, Susan. "What Rich Women Do." *MORE* Magazine. September/October 2000.

Chodorow, Nancy. *The Reproduction of Mothering*. Berkeley and Los Angeles: University of California Press, 1978.

Chodorow, Nancy. "Family Structure and Feminine Personality," in *Women, Culture and Society*, edd. M. Rosalda and L. Lamphere, Palo Alto: Stanford University Press, 1974.

Chopin, Kate. *The Awakening*, Avon reprint edition, 1994.

Clapp, Genevieve. *Divorce and New Beginnings*. New York: John Wiley & Sons, 1992.

Conlin, Michelle. "The New Debate over Working Moms." *Business Week*, September 18, 2000.

Crawford, Mary, and Rhoda Unger. *Women and Gender: A Feminist Psychology*. 3rd edition, New York: McGraw-Hill, 2000.

Delfiner, Rita, "Madonna weds amid veils of secrecy: Guy do!" *The New York Post*, December 23, 2000.

Dion, Kenneth L. and Karen K. Dion. "Romantic Love: Individual and Cultural Perspective," in Barnes and Sternberg 1988.

Dorman, Lesley. "Chat-Room Cheating?" *Redbook Magazine*, May 2000.

Dowling, Collette. *The Cinderella Complex*. New York: Summit Books, 1981.

Dwan, Shaila. "Call Me Miss (And Fabulous and Single)." *New York Times*, October 29, 2000.

References

Ehrenreich, Barbara. "In Praise of Best Friends: The Revival of a Fine Old Institution," in *Feminist Frontiers IV*, edd. L. Richardson, V. Taylor, and N. Whittier. New York: McGraw-Hill, 1997.

Estes, Clarissa Pinkola. "Women Who Run with the Wolves." *Oprah Magazine* November 2000:

Estess, Patricia Schiff. *Money Advice for Your Successful Remarriage*. Paperback edition iUniverse, 2001.

Evans, Nicholas, *The Horsewhisperer*. New York: Bantam Books, 1996.

Faludi, Susan. *Stiffed: The Betrayal of the American Male*. New York: William Morrow, 1999.

Finnerty, Amy. "The Tween Menace/Young Girls, Sophisticated Tastes." *The Wall Street Journal*, October 20, 2000.

Friday, Nancy. *My Mother, My Self*. New York: Delacorte, 1977.

Friday, Nancy. *Our Looks, Our Lives: Sex, Beauty, Power, and the Need to Be Seen*. New York: Harper Paperbacks, 1996.

Friedan, Betty. *The Feminine Mystique*. New York: Dell Publishing, 1973.

Gable, Sara, Jay Belsky, and Keith Crnic, cited in Lamanna and Riedmann 2000.

Gerhardt, Pam. "The Emotional Cost of Infidelity." *Washington Post*, March 30, 1999.

Gilligan, Carol. "Woman's Place in Man's Life Cycle," in *Psychology of Women*, ed. Juanita H. Williams. New York: W.W. Norton & Company, 1985.

Greene, Liz and Juliet Sharman-Burke. *The Mythic Journey*. New York: Fireside, 2000.

Greer, Germaine. *The Female Eunuch*. London: MacGibbon & Kee, 1970.

Grimms Brothers. *The Complete Grimms Fairy Tales*. New York: Random House, 1972.

Halcomb, Ruth. *Women Making It: Patterns and Profiles of Success*. New York: Atheneum, 1979.

Harvey, Christy. "A Guide to Who Holds the Purse Strings." *Wall Street Journal*, June 22, 2000.

Hass, Nancy. "Guess What Sells Cars? Guess Again." *New York Times*, October 12, 2000.

References

Hatfield, Elaine. "Passionate and Companionate Love," in *Harvard Women's Health Watch*, September 2000.

Hite, Shere. *The Hite Report on the Family*. New York: Grove Press, 1994.

Hite, Shere. *Women and Love: A Cultural Revolution in Progress*. New York: Alfred A. Knopf, 1987.

Hrdy, Sarah Blaffer. *Mother Nature: Material Instincts and How They Shape the Human Species*. New York: Ballantine, 1999.

Jeffreys, Nancy Ann. "The New Economic Family," in *Harvard Women's Healthwatch*, September 2000.

Kamps, Louisa. "The Pursuit of Happiness." *Elle*, October 2000.

Keats, Nancy. "The Ultimate 40th Birthday Gift." *Wall Street Journal*, October 13, 2000.

Kierkegaard, Soren. *Parables of Kierkegaard*, ed. Thomas C. Oden. Princeton NJ: Princeton University Press, 1978.

Kinsey, Alfred. *Sexual Behavior in the Human Female*. Philadelphia: W.B. Saunders, 1953.

Kimmel, Michael S. *The Gendered Society*. New York: Oxford University Press, 2000.

Lachman, Margie E. and Jacquelyn Boone James, edd. *Multiple Paths in Midlife Development*. Chicago: The University of Chicago Press, 1997.

Lamanna, Mary and Agnes Riedmann. *Marriages and Families: Making Choices in a Diverse Society*, 7th edition. Belmont CA: Wadsworth/ Thomas Learning, 2000.

Lemonick, Michael, "Teens Before Their Time." *Time* Magazine, October 30, 2000.

Lerner, Gerda. *The Creation of the Patriarchy*. New York: Oxford University Press: 1987.

Lerner, Gerda. *The Creation of Feminist Consciousness*. New York: Oxford University Press, 1993.

Lerner, Harriet. *The Dance of Anger*. New York: Harper Collins, 1997.

Levin, Ira, *Rosemary's Baby*. New York: Penguin Books, 1967.

Levinson, Daniel. *The Seasons of a Woman's Life*. New York: Ballantine Books, 1996.

MacDermid, S., Heilbrun, C. and DeHaan, L. "Employed Mothers

References

in Multiple Roles," in Lachmann and James 1997.

MacKinnon, Catherine A. "Sexuality," in *The Second Wave: A Reader in Feminist Theory*.

Masters, William H., Virginia E. Johnson, and Robert C. Kolodny. *Heterosexuality*. New York: Harper Collins, 1994.

Matousek, Mark, "Friends for Life?" *Oprah* Magazine, November 2000.

McBride, Brent A. and Thomas R. Rane. "Parenting Alliances as a Predictor of Father Involvement: An Exploratory Study," in Lamanna and Riedmann 2000.

McMurtry, Larry. *Terms of Endearment*. Touchstone reissue edition, 1989.

Mead, Margaret. *Male and Female*. New York: William Morrow, 1949.

Moore, Thomas. *Soul Mates: Honoring the Mysteries of Love and Relationship*. New York: Harper Collins Publishers, 1994.

Collins, Connie "50 Ways To Reinvent Your Life." *More* Magazine, February 2001.

Nietzsche, Friedrich. *Thus Spake Zarathustra*. Dover reprint edition, 1999.

Norris, P., ed. *Women, Media, and Politics*. New York: Oxford University Press, 1996.

Orloff, Judith. *Dr. Judith Orloff's Guide to Intuitive Healing*. New York: Random House, 2000.

Paul, Elizabeth L. "A Longitudinal Analysis of Midlife Interpersonal Relationships," in Lachman and James 1997.

Peele, Stanton. "Fools for Love: The Romantic Ideal, Psychological Theory and Addictive Love," in *The Psychology of Love*, edd. Robert J. Sternberg and Michael L. Barnes, New Haven: Yale University Press, 1988.

Peterson, Karen, cited in Lamanna and Riedmann 2000.

Rossman, Marge. *When the Headhunter Calls*. Chicago: Contemporary Books, 1981.

Schwartz, Felice N. "Management Women and the New Facts of Life." *Harvard Business Review*, June 1989.

Shapiro & Lips, cited in Lamanna and Riedmann, 2000.

References

Shapiro, Susan and Michelle Kasson. *The Men Out There: A Woman's Little Black Book*. Bethel CT: Rutledge Books, 1997.

Sheehy, Gail. *New Passages: Mapping Your Life Across Time*. New York: Ballantine Books, 1996.

Sheehy, Gail. *Understanding Men's Passages: Discovering the New Maps of Men's Lives*. New York: Ballantine Books, 1999.

Simmons, Simone. *Diana: The Secret Years*. New York: Ballantine Books, 1998.

Steinem, Gloria. *Revolution from Within*. Boston: Little Brown & Company, 1992.

Steinem, Gloria. "The Way We Were and Will Be," in *Feminism in Our Time: The Essentials Writings, World War II to the Present*, ed. Miriam Schneir. New York: Vintage Books, 1994.

Sternberg, Robert, cited in Lamanna and Riedmann 2000.

Stewart, Nathaniel. *The Effective Woman Manager*. New York: John Wiley & Sons, 1978.

Strain, Pamela Redmond. "Are You Getting in Your Own Way?" *Self Magazine*, November 2000.

Taraborelli, Randy J. *Jackie Ethel Joan: Women of Camelot*. New York: Warner Books, 2000.

Tavris, Carol. *The Mismeasure of Woman: Why Women Are Not the Better Sex, the Inferior Sex or the Opposite Sex*. New York: Touchstone Books, 1992.

Thomas, Sandra P. *Psychosocial Correlates of Physical Health*. Chicago: University of Chicago Press, 1997.

Toll, Eckhart, *The Power of Now*. Novato CA: New World Library, 1999.

Ventura, Stephanie J., cited in Lamanna and Riedmann 2000.

Waller, Robert James. *The Bridges of Madison County*. New York: Warner Books, 1997.

Walker, Alice. "Beauty: When the Other Dancer is the Self," in *Constellations: A Contextual Reader for Writers*, edd. John L. Schilb, Elizabeth Flynn and John Clifford. New York: Harper Collins, 1995.

Walsh, Mary Williams. "Seeking the Right Child-Care Formula," *New York Times*, September 13, 2000.

References

Walters, Marianne Betty Carter, Peggy Papp, and Olga Silverstein. *The Invisible Well: Gendar Patterns in Family Relationships*. New York: The Guilford Press, 1988.

Wharton, Edith, *The House of Mirth*. Signet reprint edition, 2000.

Williams, Juanita, ed. *The Psychology of Women*. New York: W.W. Norton & Company, 1985.

Woodman, Maryann. *Addiction to Perfection: The Still Unravished Bride*. Toronto: Inner City Books, 1982.

www.women.com. Survey, January 1999.

www.womeningovernment.com.

Yager, Jan. *Friendshifts: The Power of Friendship and How It Shapes Our Lives*. Stamford CT: Hannacroix Creek Books, 1997.